Practical Traditional
Chinese Medicine &
Pharmacology

Acupuncture and Moxibustion

By Geng Junying and Su Zhihong

New World Press, Beijing

First Edition 1991
Third Printing 1998

ISBN 7-80005-115-3

Published by
NEW WORLD PRESS
24 Baiwanzhuang Road, Beijing 100037, China

Distributed by
NEW WORLD PRESS
Tel: 0086-10-68326645

Printed in the People's Republic of China

CONTENTS

I

III

IV

Preface

This series of "Practical Traditional Chinese Medicine and Pharmacology" consists of five separate books: *Basic Theories and Principles; Acupuncture and Moxibustion; Medicinal Herbs; Herbal Formulas;* and *Clinical Experiences.* These books represent a comprehensive and systematic treatment of the theories and practices of traditional Chinese medicine and pharmacology. This series incorporates a practical approach to the study of Chinese medicine through its use of simple explanations and thorough outlines.

In the first volume, *Basic Theories and Principles,* the *Yin-Yang* and Five Elements theories are addressed as the basic philosophical elements of traditional Chinese medicine. The theories of physiology, pathology, etiology, diagnostic methodology, and syndrome differentiation in traditional Chinese medicine are explained in a discussion of the *zang-fu* organs (the internal organs) and channels-collaterals. These theories stress the importance of the appropriate holistic treatment according to an accurate diagnosis of the particular complaint. Thus the reader can learn the methods of understanding disease using the vantage point of traditional Chinese medicine and also command a knowledge of its basic theories.

The second volume, *Acupuncture and Moxibustion,* introduces techniques of acupuncture and moxibustion, commonly used acupuncture points, basic laws and methods of selecting points, and

1

details of acupuncture treatment of the common diseases as described in an appendix of typical cases. It enables the reader to learn not only acupuncture techniques for more than forty kinds of diseases and symptoms, but also methods of selecting appropriate points for different symptoms.

The third and fourth volumes, *Medicinal Herbs* and *Herbal Formulas,* provide exhaustive and practicable information on individual traditional Chinese medicinal herbs, and formulas of medicinal herbs. The former presents the theory of the Four Properties and Five Flavors of herbal drugs, the theory of ascending and descending, floating and sinking, and direction of action of medicinal herbs. Also discussed is a description of the origin, property, flavor, and classification of three hundred herbs according to their therapeutic action on diseases of specific channels, general therapeutic action, indications, dispensation of herbal prescription, and contraindications. Readers will learn in the fourth volume the original source and ingredients of one hundred fifty commonly used herbal formulas, and their therapeutic actions, indications, and contraindications. By bringing theories, methods, prescriptions, and individual herbs together, they reflect the philosophy of traditional Chinese medicine which applies treatment on the basis of syndrome differentiation. Readers will not only become acquainted with one hundred fifty commonly used herbal formulas, but also with the laws and methods of differentiating syndromes, the principles of constructing herbal prescriptions, and other aspects of traditional Chinese herbal medicine.

The fifth volume, *Clinical Experiences,* introduces therapeutic methods of treating common internal disease, gynecology, and pediatrics. It associates practical application of theories, methods, herbal formulas, and individual herbs with clinical methods. Moreover, readers can use the fifth volume to learn the basic methods of applying treatment according to syndrome differentiation using the theories of traditional Chinese medicine and pharmacology.

This series on traditional Chinese medicine has been compiled by professionals with many years of experience in teaching, scientific research, and clinical treatment. Each volume has been checked and approved by leading authorities in the field of traditional Chinese medicine and pharmacology. These books present the reader with an easy access to state of the art knowledge on Chinese traditional medicine and pharmacology. The information presented in this series is the product of years of combined research and provides a reference for beginners as well as professionals in the field of traditional medicine. At present it is rare to read English editions which completely and systematically introduce traditional Chinese medical philosophies and methodologies with such conciseness. We hope that this series is able to involve interested readers from all over the world in the development and dissemination of this ancient art for the benefit of the human race.

Professor Dong Jianhua

Director of the All-China Association of
Traditional Chinese Medicine
Advisor to the Public Health Ministry of
the People's Republic of China

Introduction

Acupuncture and Moxibustion, one of the five books in the Practical Traditional Chinese Medicine and Pharmacology series, is intended to acupuncture practitioners and students. Instead of expounding largely and copiously on acupuncture theories and principles, we stressed in the book more on its practical value and applicability than theoretical explorations. It is mainly of our personal experiences accumulated from years of teaching and clinical practice.

The book is divided into three chapters. The first chapter introduces the most essential and practical techniques as well as the points which merit special attention in applying acupuncture treatments. The second chapter is devoted to the most commonly used acupoints. With a view to practicability and convenience, we have not only explained the location, function, pathological indications of each point as almost all books on acupuncture do, but also provided detailed information on the main points to be combined with the current point in treating different types of diseases as well as point variations for the different syndromes of the same disease. Notes are made also to the needling method for each point. The third chapter deals with acupuncture treatments of common diseases. Again in order to make the book more practical and convenient for clinical use, we did not follow the conventional practice of merely mentioning the syndromes

4

and listing the points. Instead we first differentiated each case to determine the nature of its syndrome type as a doctor of traditional Chinese medicine would have done in the clinic. That is to determine whether the syndromes are of the *yin, yang, xu,* or *shi* type. Then different methods as well as their purpose and functions are suggested for each type. We personally used all these treatments and found them very effective. In fact, so wonderfully effective are some of the methods that the patients thought we had played magic on them. Case studies are given to the specially effective cases.

We sincerely hope it will be of help to those who work in this field.

Chapter I

ACUPUNCTURE AND MOXIBUSTION

Acupuncture and moxibustion are different methods of treating diseases, involving the use of needles or the application of heat produced by ignited objects, to stimulate certain points or loci on the body. This chapter deals with the manipulation of the filiform needle and the use of moxibustion.

Section One

Acupuncture Needling Techniques

1. The Needles

The most popular acupuncture needles are the filiform needle, the cutaneous needle (including the plum-blossom needle or seven-star needle) and the three-edged needle.

The most commonly used filiform needles vary in length

7

from 0.5 to 5 *cun** (1.67-16.67 cm), and the diameter of the body from Gauge No. 34 to No. 26.

Cutaneous needles are used to stimulate the skin superficially. The most common varieties are the plum-blossom and seven-star needles (*Fig.* 1-2).

The seven-star needle is composed of seven short stainless steel needles inlaid onto a small round plate attached vertically to a handle, like a hammer, while the plum-blossom needle is composed of five such needles, arranged like the petals of the plum-flower.

Good results can be obtained by using this method of treatment in cases of local areas of inflammation, neuralgia, and arthritic pain.

Tapping may be light, medium or heavy. When treating children or patients who are very weak, a relatively mild method of stimulation is indicated. When the skin becomes red and warm, needling should be stopped. Conversely patients who have acute or chronic inflammation, such as obstinate tinea and erysipelas, may be stimulated more vigorously. The skin should become red and slight bleeding occur. Medium stimulation is tapping, causing local congestion. This method of tapping is most popular.

The head of the three-edged needle is triangular in shape, with a sharp tip (*Fig.* 1-3).

The three-edged needle is used to prick and cause bloodletting.

2. Preparations

Position

A position should be chosen for the patient, which allows the physician access to the points to be needled, and is comfortable for the patient. The most commonly used positions are sitting and lying (*Fig.* 1-4).

Sterilization

Strict sterilization of the needle is imperative. The areas of

---

* *Cun*: a unit of length (= 1/3 decimeter).

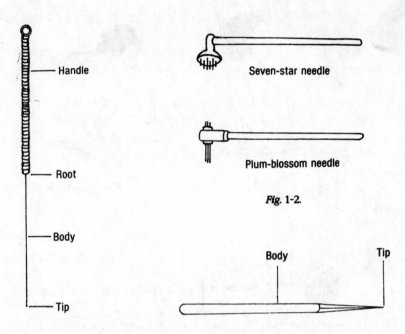

Seven-star needle

Plum-blossom needle

Fig. 1-2.

Body   Tip

Handle

Root

Body

Tip

Fig. 1-1. The filiform needle.   *Fig.* 1-3. The three-edged needle.

skin around points selected on the patient should be cleaned with 75 percent alcohol and 1.5 percent iodine. Strict sterilization should becarried out during the whole operation.

Inspection

Prior to use, a needle should be inspected to see that no burrs, stains or tiny cracks have appeared on it. If there is anything wrong, the needle must be discarded to avoid accident.

3. Manipulation of the Filiform Needle

The Method, Angle and Depth of Needle Insertion

According to the location of the point and the size of the

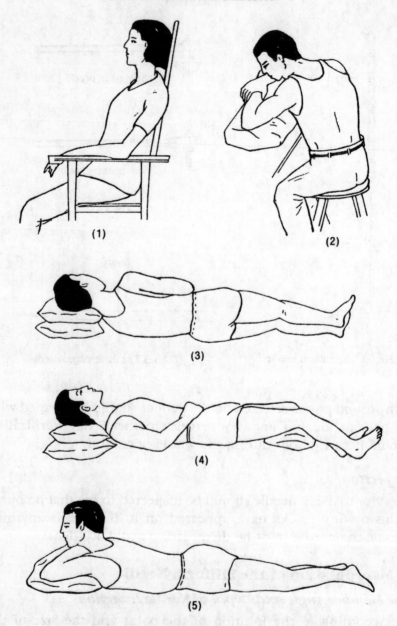

Fig. 1-4. The most commonly used positions for needling.

needle, there are various methods of insertion, such as thumbnail assisted insertion, holding needle handle and body insertion, pinching skin insertion, and pulling skin taut insertion, etc.Whatever method is used, quick and accurate insertion is required. Generally, the thumbnail assisted insertion is suitable for puncturing with short needles; the holding needle handle and body insertion is suitable for long needles; the pinching skin insertion is suitable for puncturing points of the thin tissue; the pulling skin taut insertion is indicated for points where the skin is loose and flabby (*Fig.* 1-5).

Angle: Generally, there are three angles for insertion:

1) Perpendicular, in which the needle is inserted perpendicularly forming a 90-degree angle with the skin surface. Most points on the body can be punctured perpendicularly.

2) Oblique, in which the needle is inserted obliquely to form an angle of 45 degrees with the skin surface. This method is indicated for points located where the muscle is thin or close to important viscera.

3) Transverse, in which the needle is inserted transversely to form an angle of 15 degrees with the skin surface. This method is preferred for points which have very little underlying muscle.

Appropriate depth of insertion is important. The best way is to give the patient needle sensation but not to hurt him (*Fig.* 1-6).

Obtaining Qi (Needling Reaction) and the Method of Insertion

When the needle is inserted to a certain depth, the patient may feel soreness, numbness or distention around the point, while the operator may feel tenseness around the needle. This is called the "arrival" of Qi. The method used to obtain Qi is called the manipulation of the needle. The needling reaction is the basis for acupuncture therapy. Without it, good results cannot be obtained. Two methods that will obtain Qi or increase the stimulation are the vibrating method, which is to raise and thrust the needle with strong or mild stimulation, and the rotating method, which is to rotate the needle back and forth.

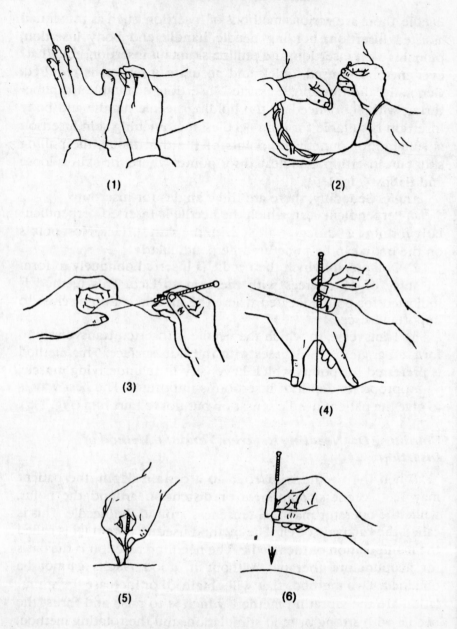

(1)

(2)

(3)

(4)

(5)

(6)

Fig. 1-5. Methods of needle insertion.

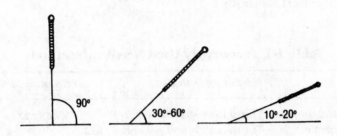

Fig. 1-6. Angles of needle insertion.

The Reinforcing and Reducing Method

The effects of the reinforcing and reducing of needling are closely connected with three factors:

1) *The State of the Organism* Different manifestations of the effect may appear in different pathological conditions. One instance is the lowering of blood pressure in a patient with hypertension, and raising it in hypotension. Similarly, needling Zusanli (St. 36) may have a spasmolytic effect on intestinal spasm, while promoting peristalsis in intestinal paralysis.

2) *The Function of the Acupuncture Point* The effect of reinforcing and reducing manipulation is connected with therapeutic properties of the points. Needling Guanyuan (Ren 4), Qihai (Ren 6), Zusanli (St. 36), Mingmen (Du 4), and Shenshu (U.B. 23) will have a reinforcing effect in promoting functional activity. On the other hand, a reducing effect may be obtained by pricking Shixuan (Extra), Weizhong (U.B. 40), Quchi (L.I. 11) in order to bring down fever and expel the excess of pathological factor. Moreover some points, such as Neiguan (P. 6) and Hegu (L.I. 4), may have either effect. The former is effective in both inducing and relieving nausea, while the latter can induce and relieve perspiration.

3) *Needling Methods* Reinforcing and reducing are connected not only with the state of the organism and the needling points,

but also with the operator. Below is a table of some of the frequently used methods:

Table 1-1 Frequently Used Needling Methods

Name	Reinforcing Methods	Reducing Methods
Raising and thrusting the needle	Thrust from shallow to deep. Thrust heavily and raise gently in a small range and at low speed.	Vice versa
Rotating the needle	Thrust and rotate gently and slowly in a small range.	Vice versa
Even movement	Thrust evenly and gently at a moderate speed. Rotate and withdraw after Qi is obtained.	

The methods mentioned above can be used alone or coordinately with either of the two. Of the two, the Even Movement is more popular.

Retaining and Withdrawing the Needle

Whether the needle should be retained after Qi is obtained depends on the needs of the treatment and the points being punctured. Generally, when the puncture points Yamen (Du 15), Lianquan (Ren 23), Tiantu (Ren 22), and Jing-Well points are used, the needle should not be retained; this is also true in urgent cases of shock or unconsciousness.

To prevent bleeding at the site of puncture, it is necessary to raise the needle gently before withdrawing it quickly; press the puncture site gently with a cotton ball upon withdrawal.

Management of Possible Accidents in Acupuncture

Fainting: This may occur due to weakness or nervous tension on receiving acupuncture for the first time, or to too forceful manipulation. The prodromes are dizziness and vertigo, irritability, nausea, pallor, staring eyes and dull appearance. In severe cases there may be shock, unconsciousness, or hypotension. The needles should be removed at once and the patient asked to relax. The operator should help him to lie down. Warm or sweet water may be given. The symptoms will disappear after a short rest in mild cases. In severe cases, puncture Renzhong (Du 26), Suliao (Du 25), and Zusanli (St. 36). Moxibustion may be applied to Baihui (Du 20), Qihai (Ren 6) or Guanyuan (Ren 4). Other emergency measures should be taken if the patient still fails to respond.

Precautionary measures to be taken against fainting are suggested according to the individual. Patients receiving acupuncture for the first time should be punctured gently; those who are very weak, tired or hungry should not be punctured; those who have walked a long way should be encouraged to rest for a time before treatment. It is usually a good idea to have such patients lie down for treatment, to avoid fainting.

Stuck needle: The needle may become stuck in place, difficult to manipulate or withdraw. This is often caused by an extremely nervous patient. A stuck needle often loosens when the area around it is massaged. If the needle still cannot be withdrawn, another point nearby should be punctured to relieve the muscle tension.

Bent needle: When a needle bends beneath the skin, do not twirl or rotate it as it is withdrawn. The position of the patient should be changed and the needle should be withdrawn in accordance with its angle. Forcing the needle may cause it to break.

Broken needle: When a break is discovered, it is important that the physician remain calm and that the patient be kept still, so that the broken needle does not go deeper. If part of the broken needle protrudes from the skin, forceps or tweezers may be used to extract it. If it has broken in deep tissue, the needle fragment

15

must be removed surgically. To prevent accident, careful inspection of the needle should be made, and it should not be inserted to its full length.

Hematoma: After withdrawal of the needle, a red pin-point mark may remain. This is considered normal, and it will disappear of itself.

Section Two

Moxibustion

Moxibustion is a method whereby a certain object is burned on or above the skin at acupuncture points. The most popular material for moxibustion is "moxa-wool" (dried pulverized leaves of the Chinese mugwort plant—*Artemisiae Argyi*). The popular methods of using it are moxa-stick, moxa-cones and warming needle.

Moxibustion with Moxa: Simply roll moxa-wool into the shape of a stick. Apply a lighted moxa-stick over the selected point. According to different manipulating of the moxa-stick, it may be called mild warmth method and sparrow feeding method (*Fig.* 1-7).

Moxibustion with Moxa-Cones: The moxa-wool is shaped into little cones that are placed directly on the skin at selected points and burned. A medium place between the burning moxa and the skin is the distinction between direct and indirect moxibustion. Direct moxibustion may be scarring or non-scarring, giving blisters or none. Indirect moxibustion may be classified according to the different substances insulating the cone and the skin, such as garlic, ginger and salt (*Fig.* 1-8).

Warming needle: Press the moxa-wool on the needle handle and ignite it. This method is suitable for combined treatment of puncturing and moxibustion (*Fig.* 1-9).

16

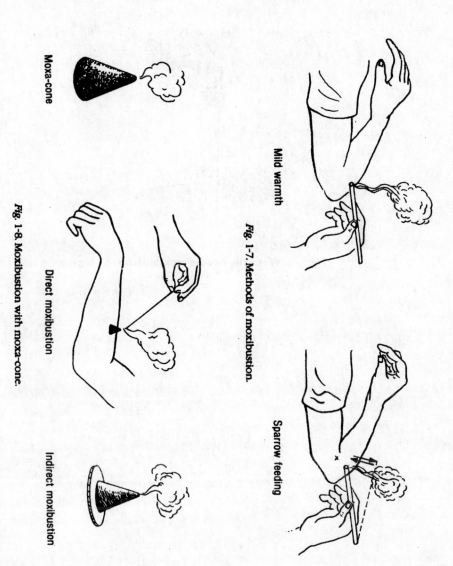

Mild warmth

Sparrow feeding

Fig. 1-7. Methods of moxibustion.

Moxa-cone

Direct moxibustion

Indirect moxibustion

Fig. 1-8. Moxibustion with moxa-cone.

Fig. 1-9. Warming needle moxibustion.

Chapter II

ACUPUNCTURE POINTS

Section One

The Classification of Acupuncture Points

Acupuncture points consist of three kinds:

1. Channel Points

All the points located along the paths of the fourteen regular channels are called the channel points, or the fourteen channel points.

2. Off-Channel Points or Extraordinary Points

All those that are not located along the paths of the fourteen channels but have their certain names and locations are called off-channel points, such as Taiyang (Extra), Yintang (Extra), etc.

3. Points of Pain or Ashi Points

Those that have no fixed names or locations but get pain

19

when palpated called points of pain (Chinese call these "Ah, it is point"). *Neijing* (Canon of Yellow Emperor's Internal Medicine) describes them: "Where there is a painful spot, there is an acupuncture point."

Section Two

The Location and Measurement of Acupuncture Points

1. According to Anatomical Landmarks

The points can be located according to the anatomical landmarks on the body surface.

1) The Fixed Landmarks: These include the border of nail, hairline, orifices of the five sense organs, nipple, muscle, umbilicus, vertebra, joint, depression and prominence. For instance, Tianshu (St. 25) is located two *cun* lateral to the navel. Shaoshang (Lu. 11) is located on the inner side of the thumb.

2) The Movable landmarks: These include the crease on the skin above the joints, depression in the muscle and tendons, which become visible when moved.

2. Proportional Measurement

This method is provided by the length of certain part of the body to give a standard of measurement defined in terms of *cun* and tenths of a *cun*. When locating points from physical landmarks, a system of unit measurement is applied. The length of the unit is relative to the physical proportions of the individual. Therefore this is suitable for either the adult or child.

3. Finger Measurement

The length and breadth of the patient's fingers are used as a criterion for locating points. The doctor may also do the measurement if he has a size similar to his patient's. The commonly used measuring methods are as follows:

Table 2-1 Popular Body Measurement

Part	Location	Unit (*cun*)	Captions
Head	Between front and back	12	If the posterior
	Between front hairline and eyebrow	3	hairline is indistinguishable, the distance
	Between back hairline and process of 7th cervical vertebra	3	from eyebrow to process of 7th cervical vertebra is 18 *cun*
	Between angles of hairline	9	The distance between the two mastoid processes is 9 *cun*.
Chest and abdomen	Between nipples	8	Measurement of the chest
	Between xiphisternal junction and umbilicus	8	is based on the intercostal space, each is
	Between umbilicus and the upper symphysis pubis	5	1.6 *cun*.
	Between axillary and 11th rib	12	
Back	Between scapula and the middle	3	This is based on the spinous processes of the vertebral column.
Upper extremities	Between axillary and cubital creases	9	The measurement is applicable to both the medial
	Between cubital and carpal creases	12	and the lateral aspect of the upper extremities.
Lower extremities	Between greater trochanter and middle of popliteal crease	19	The measurement is applicable to front, lateral, side and back
	Between middle of popliteal crease and lateral malleolus	16	of the lower extremities.
	Between pubis and medial epicondyle of femur	18	
	Between medial condyle of tibia and medial malleolus	13	

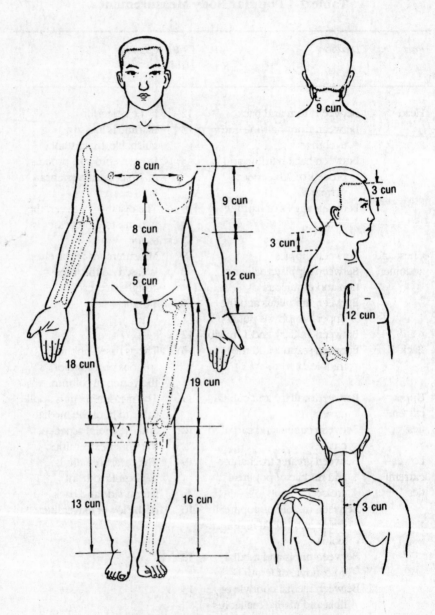

Fig. 2-1. **Proportional measurement.**

1) Measuring with the Middle Finger

When the middle finger is fixed, the distance between the two ends of the creases of the interphalangeal joints is taken as one *cun*.

2) Measuring with the Thumb

The breadth of the thumb at the middle joint is one *cun*.

3) Measuring with Four Fingers

The breadth of four fingers placed side by side, and measured at the distal joint, is three *cun* (*Fig*. 2-2).

This method is simpler but not as accurate as the proportional measurement.

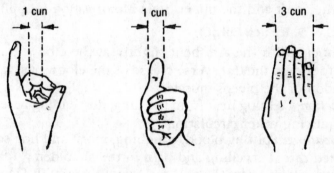

Fig. 2-2. Measuring with fingers.

Section Three

The Commonly Used Acupuncture Points

1. Points of the Lung Channel of Hand-Taiyin

Zhongfu (Lu. 1, Front-Mu Point)

Location: 6 *cun* lateral to the Ren Channel, at the lateral side of the first intercostal space.

Function: Spreading Qi of the lung, soothing asthma, and

stopping cough.

Indications: Pain in the chest, cough, asthma and fullness sensation of the chest.

Points combination: Zhongfu (Lu. 1) combined with Lieque (Lu. 7), Feishu (U.B. 13): cough and asthma; with Taixi (K. 3), Taiyuan (Lu. 9), Zusanli (St. 36), Feishu (U.B. 13): cough caused by pulmonary tuberculosis; with Neiguan (P. 6) and Yingchuang (St. 16): fullness, distension and pain of the chest; with Wuyi (St. 15), Shencang (K. 25) and Yutang (Ren 18): costal chondritis.

Method: Puncture obliquely and superior-laterally for about 1-15 *cun* with a local sensation of soreness and distension radiating to the chest and the upper limb. Moxibustion is applicable.

Chize (Lu. 5, He-Sea Point)

Location: With the arm bent slightly at the elbow, this point can be found on the transverse crease of the elbow, just lateral to the tendon of the biceps muscle.

Function: Clearing heat from the lung, descending reversed Qi and regulating water circulation.

Indications: Spitting blood, coughing, moist and hot, sore and congested throat, swelling and pain in the shoulder.

Points combination: Chize (Lu. 5) combined with Lieque (Lu. 7) and Feishu (U.B. 13): cough and asthma; with Weizhong (U.B. 40): heatstroke or sunstroke, cholera, vomiting and diarrhea; with Shaoshang (Lu. 11) and Hegu (L.I. 4): infantile fevers and convulsion; with Quchi (L.I. 11) and Hegu (L.I. 4): flaccid wrist.

Lieque (Lu. 7, Luo-Connecting Point)

Location: Proximal to the styloid process of the radius, 1.5 *cun* above the transverse crease of the wrist, in a small hollow.

Function: Spreading and regulating Lung Qi, dispersing wind and relieving exterior syndromes, removing sore throat and promoting intestinal peristalsis.

Indications: One-side headache, coughing and asthma, sore and congested throat, toothache, deviated eye and mouth.

Points combination: Lieque (Lu. 7) combined with Houxi (S.I. 3): pain of head and neck regions; with Xiaguan (St. 6), Yifeng

(S.J. 17) and Sibai (St. 2): trigeminal neuralgia; with Hegu (L.I. 4) and Dazhui (Du 14): chills and fever of common cold; Zhaohai (K. 6) soreness and swelling of the throat, stuffiness and fullness of the chest; with Zhaohai (K. 7), Zusanli (St. 36) and Yinlingquan (Sp. 9): diabetes; with Yingxiang (L.I. 20): running nose, and nasal obstruction.

Method: Slanted insertion upward, 0.5-1 *cun*.

Sensation: Local distension or extending towards the elbow.

Taiyuan (Lu. 9, Shu-Stream and Yuan-Source Point, and the Influential Point of vessels and pulses)

Location: At the transverse crease of the palmar aspect of the wrist, on the radial side of the radial artery.

Function: Clearing the lung, regulating the Qi circulation, stopping cough, improving the sore throat, removing the obstruction of the channel.

Indications: Cough, asthma, pain and stuffiness of the chest, irritability, restlessness, excessive sputum, chills and fever, hemoptysis, dry throat, pain in the shoulder, the upper back and the clavicular fossa, breast pain, rough pulse, pulseless syndrome.

Points combination: Taiyuan (Lu. 9) combined with Renying (St. 9), Chize (Lu. 5) and Neiguan (P. 6): pulseless syndrome; with Lieque (Lu. 7), Chize (Lu. 5) and Fengmen (U.B. 12): cough with sputum caused by pathogenic wind and cold; with Neiguan (P. 6) and Shenfeng (K. 23): fullness, distension and pain in the chest; with Neiting (St. 44): distending pain of the breast; with Neiguan (P. 6) and Sifeng (Extra): whooping cough.

Method: Puncture perpendicularly 0.3-0.5 *cun* avoiding the artary, local sensation of soreness and distension felt by the patient. Moxibustion is advisable.

Shaoshang (Lu. 11, Jing-Well Point)

Location: Approximately 0.1 *cun* from the base of the cuticle on the inside of the thumb.

Function: Clearing the lung, relieving sore throat, resuscitating from coma.

Indications: Sore throat, coughing, stroke, fainting.

Points combination: Shaoshang (Lu. 11) combined with Renzhong (Du 26) and Yongquan (K. 1): unconsciousness due to wind-stroke; with other Jing-Well points: consistent high fever; with Shangyang (L.I. 1): soreness and swelling of the throat, whooping cough; with Tiantu (Ren 22) and Fengmen (U.B. 12): cough with digestive problems; pricking Shaoshang (Lu. 11) to let blood out together with puncturing Hegu (L.I. 4): acute tonsillitis.

Method: Straight insertion, 1 *cun*, or prick the point with a three-edged needle, drawing a few drops of blood.

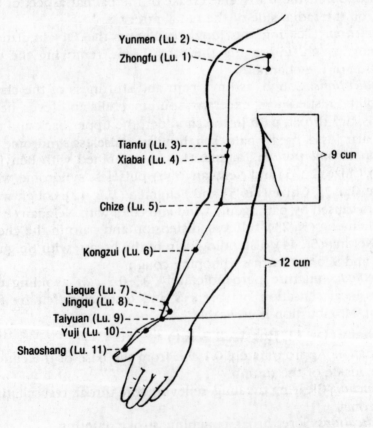

Yunmen (Lu. 2)

Zhongfu (Lu. 1)

Tianfu (Lu. 3)

Xiabai (Lu. 4)

9 cun

Chize (Lu. 5)

Kongzui (Lu. 6)

12 cun

Lieque (Lu. 7)

Jingqu (Lu. 8)

Taiyuan (Lu. 9)

Yuji (Lu. 10)

Shaoshang (Lu. 11)

Fig. 2-3. The Lung Channel of Hand-Taiyin.

2. Points of the Large Intestine Channel of Hand-Yangming

Hegu (L.I. 4, Yuan-Source Point)

Location: Between the 1st and 2nd metacarpal bones, slightly to the middle of the latter (*Fig. 2-4*).

Function: Dispersing wind, clearing heat, opening orifices, resuscitating from unconsciousness, removing obstruction from the channels and activating the circulation of Qi and blood in the vessels.

Indications: Toothache, congested and sore throat, cold, fever, headache, stuffy nose, nose blockage, eye diseases, facial paralysis or spasm, non-sweating or perspiration, paralysis of the upper limbs.

Points combination: Hegu (L.I. 4) combined with Jiache (St. 6): toothache; with Renzhong (Du 26): coma of wind-stroke; with Dicang (St. 4) and Jiache (St. 6): facial paralysis; with Fengchi (G.B. 20), Shangjuxu (St. 37) and Tianshu (St. 25): enteritis, dysentery and abdominal pain; with Fengchi (G.B. 20), Dazhui (Du 14), Quchi (L.I. 11) and Taiyang (Extra): fever and headache of common cold.

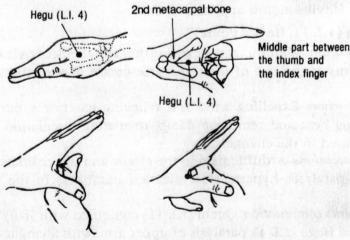

Fig. 2-4.

27

Method: Straight insertion, 0.5-1 *cun*. Join to Houxi (S.I. 3).

Sensation: local distension and soreness, or extending towards the figertips. Moxibustion may be applied for 5-10 minutes. Not advised for pregnant women.

Shousanli (L.I. 10)

Location: 2 *cun* below Quchi (L.I. 11), on the connecting line between Yangxi (L.I. 5) and Quchi (L.I. 11).

Function: Dispelling pathogenic wind, removing obstruction from the channels, regulating the circulation of Qi and harmonizing the middle Jiao.

Indications: Deviated mouth and eyes, toothache, mumps, swollen cheeks, pain of shoulder and arm, difficult extension of elbow and hand, numbness and paralysis of the upper limb, abdominal pain, diarrhea, carbuncles.

Points combination: Shousanli (L.I. 10) combined with Quchi (L.I. 11), Tianjing (S.J. 10) and Shaohai (H. 3): spasm and difficult extension of elbow; with Jiache (St. 6): toothache; with Hegu (L.I. 4) and Yanglao (S.I. 6): furuncles and carbuncles; with Zusanli (St. 36): disorders of the stomach and intestines.

Method: Puncture perpendicularly 1-2 *cun*. With a local sensation of soreness and distension radiating to the dorsum of the hand. Moxibustion is applicable.

Quchi (L.I. 11, He-Sea Point)

Location: With the arm flexed at the lateral epicondyle of the humerus at the end of the transverse crease of the elbow (*Fig. 2-5*).

Function: Expelling wind and relieving exterior syndromes; clearing heat and removing damp, regulating circulation of Qi and blood in the channels.

Indications: Arthritic pain in the elbow and upper limbs, high fever, paralysis, hypertension, measles, numbness in the upper limbs.

Points combination: Quchi (L.I. 11) combined with Jianyu (L.I. 15) and Hegu (L.I. 4): paralysis of upper arm; with Shangjuxu (St. 37): dysentery and enteritis; with Dazhui (Du 14): anti-fever; with

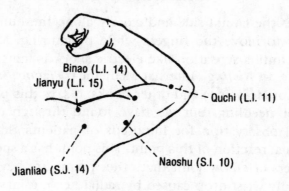

Fig. 2-5.

Shousanli (L.I. 10) and Renying (St. 9): hypertension; with Xuehai (Sp. 10): urticaria and itching of skin; with Sanyinjiao (Sp. 6): irregular menstruation; with Hegu (L.I. 4): sore throat; with Shenmen (H. 7) and Yuji (Lu. 10): hematemesis.

Method: Straight insertion, 1-1.5 *cun*. For hypertension, join with Shaohai (H. 3).

Sensation: Local distension and soreness, or distended sensation expending towards the fingers and the shoulders.

Hand-Wuli (L.I. 13)

Location: 3 *cun* above Quchi (L.I. 11), on the line connecting Quchi (L.I. 11) and Jianyu (L.I. 15).

Function: Relaxing the tendons, relieving Wei syndromes, removing stasis and stopping pain.

Indications: Pain spasm and inability of extension of shoulder and elbow paralysis and numbness of the upper limb, scrofula, and hand drop.

Points combination: Hand-Wuli (L.I. 13) combined with Quchi (L.I. 11), Shaohai (H. 3) and Quze (P. 3): spasm, pain and inability of extension of elbow joint; with Binao (L.I. 14), Jianyu (L.I. 15) and Quze (P. 3): difficult raising up and pain of the shoulder; with Hegu (L.I. 4), Chize (Lu. 5), Jianyu (L.I. 15) and Jiquan (H. 1): numbness and paralysis of the upper limb; with Shousanli (L.I. 10) and Zhigou (S.J. 6): wrist drop.

Method: Puncture obliquely 1.5-2 *cun* from the medial side towards the lateral side and closely along the humerus. Ask the patient to move the fingers while puncturing. Manipulate the needle until a sensation like electric shock is felt by the patient.

Note: In *Neijing* (Internal Medicine), *Yizong Jinjian* (Golden Mirror of Medicine) and other books, it says this point is forbidden for needling. But we have found through our long time clinical observation for hundreds of patients that there is no abnormal reaction of this point. This point has a special effect for disorders of elbow joint that other points are beyond compare, especially wrist drop caused by radial nerve injury, and difficult extension and flexion of fingers caused by hemiplegia.

Jianyu (L.I. 15)

Location: At the top of the shoulder. When the arm is inducted parallel to the ground, this point can be found in a distinct depression just in front of the shoulder (See *Fig.* 2-5).

Function: Activating the circulation of blood, stopping pain, and relieving joint pain.

Indications: Arthritic pain in shoulder, paralysis, numbness and pain in the upper limb.

Points combination: Jianyu (L.I. 15) combined with Jianliao (S.J. 14) and Jugu (L.I. 16): shoulder joint pain; with Quchi (L.I. 11): frozen shoulder; with Yanglingquan (G.B. 34) and Jianliao (S.J. 14): supra-acromial bursitis.

Method: Straight insertion, 1-2 *cun* towards Jiquan (H. 1), or slanted insertion downward, 1-3 *cun* with arm hanging freely at the side.

Neck-Futu (L.I. 18)

Location: Level with the Adam's apple between the sternal head and clavicular head of m. sternocleidomastoideus.

Function: Stopping pain, subsidence of swelling, spreading the lung Qi.

Indications: Stiffness and pain of the head and neck, soreness and swelling of throat, aphonia, cough, asthma with wheezing, goiter, neuralgia of major and minor auricular nerves.

Points combination: Neck-Futu (L.I. 18) combined with Tiantu

(Ren 22) and Taixi (K. 3): sputum gurgling on the throat, cough and asthma; with Hegu (L.I. 4): pain and soreness of throat; with Tiantu (Ren 22), Lianquan (Ren 23) and Taichong (Liv. 3): aphonia; with Shuitu (St. 10), Hegu (L.I. 4) and Tiantu (Ren 22): goiter; with Yifeng (S.J. 17): neuralgia of major auricular nerve; with Fengchi (G.B. 20) and Hand-Wangu (S.I. 4): neuralgia of minor occipital nerve.

Method: Puncture perpendicularly 0.5-0.8 *cun*. Moxibustion is advisable. Puncture obliquely and supra-laterally 0.5-1.2 *cun* for neuralgia of major auricular nerve. With a sensation of soreness and numbness spreading to the ear. Puncture obliquely and supra-medially 0.8-1 *cun* with a sensation of distension and heaviness in the throat for sore throat and aphonia. Puncture obliquely and infra-posteriorly 1-1.5 *cun* with a sensation of soreness and distension of the lateral aspect of the neck for twitching of the shoulder and stiffness, pain and motor impairment of the neck.

Yingxiang (L.I. 20)

Location: 0.5 *cun* to the nostril, in the nasolabial sulcus (*Fig.* 2-6).

Function: Dispersing wind, clearing heat and removing obstruction of the nose.

Indications: Rhinitis, nasosinusitis, facial paralysis, round worm in the bile duct.

Points combination: Yingxiang (L.I. 20) combined with Fengchi (G.B. 20) and Hegu (L.I. 4): epistaxis; with Shangxing (Du 23) and Yintang (Extra): rhinitis; with Renzhong (Du 26): swelling and itching of face; with Quchi (L.I. 11), Fengchi (G.B. 20) and Waiguan (S.J. 5): nasal obstruction and running nose due to common cold.

Method: Transverse insertion, directed up inward 0.3 to 0.5 *cun*. For round worm of the bile duct, transverse insertion jointed to Sibai (St. 2).

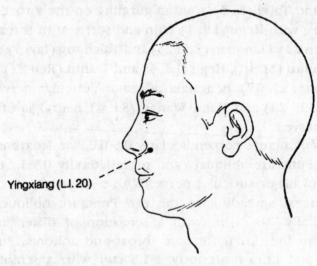

Yingxiang (L.I. 20)

Fig. 2-6.

3. Points of the Stomach Channel of Foot-Yangming

Chengqi (St. 1)

Location: Directly below the pupil of the eye, between the interior border of the orbit and the eyeball (*Fig.* 2-8).

Function: Dispersing the wind, activating the circulation of blood in the channels, opening the orifices and brightening the vision.

Indications: Myopia, pain of the nerve of the orbit. *Points combination*: Chengqi (St. 1) combined with Fenglong (St. 40), Fuai (Sp. 16) and Fushe (Sp. 13): constipation; with Fengchi (G.B. 20) and Shenmen (H. 7): insomnia; with Tiantu (Ren 22), Fengmen (U.B. 12), Zhongwan (Ren 12), Chize (Lu. 5) and Zusanli (St. 36): asthma with excessive sputum; with Feishu (U.B. 13) and Xiongxiang (Sp. 19): cough; with Fuliu (K. 7): edema of limbs.

Method: Puncture perpendicularly 0.5-1.0 *cun* with a sensation of soreness and distension.

Sibai (St. 2)

Location: Approximately 1 *cun* directly below the pupil of the eye, at the infra-orbital foramen.

Function: Expelling wind, removing obstruction from the

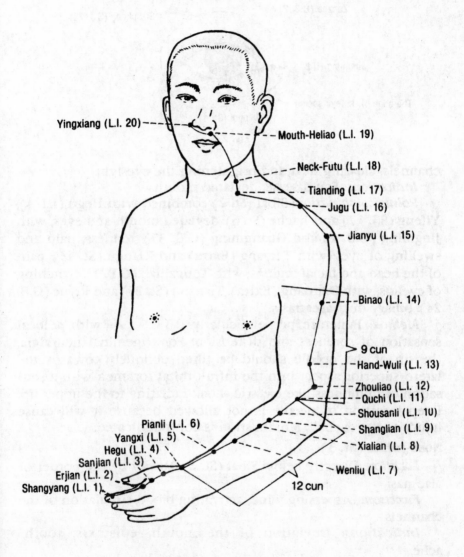

Yingxiang (L.I. 20)
Mouth-Heliao (L.I. 19)
Neck-Futu (L.I. 18)
Tianding (L.I. 17)
Jugu (L.I. 16)
Jianyu (L.I. 15)
Binao (L.I. 14)
9 cun
Hand-Wuli (L.I. 13)
Zhouliao (L.I. 12)
Quchi (L.I. 11)
Shousanli (L.I. 10)
Shanglian (L.I. 9)
Xialian (L.I. 8)
Wenliu (L.I. 7)
12 cun
Pianli (L.I. 6)
Yangxi (L.I. 5)
Hegu (L.I. 4)
Sanjian (L.I. 3)
Erjian (L.I. 2)
Shangyang (L.I. 1)

Fig. 2-7. The Large Intestine Channel of Hand-Yangming.

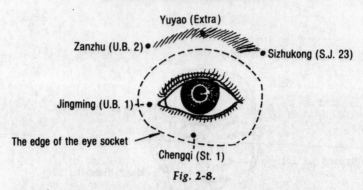

Fig. 2-8.

channels, clearing heat and brightening the eyesight.

Indications: Eye disease, deviated mouth.

Points combination: Sibai (St. 2) combined with Hegu (L.I. 4), Yifeng (S.J. 17) and Jiache (St. 6): deviated mouth and eyes; with Jingming (U.B. 1) and Guangming (G.B. 37): redness, pain and swelling of eyes; with Taiyang (Extra) and Xiangu (St. 43): pain of the head and facial regions; with Tongziliao (G.B. 1): twitching of eyelids; with Dannang (Extra), Tianshu (St. 25) and Riyue (G.B. 24): biliary duct ascariasis.

Method: Puncture perpendicularly 0.3-0.5 *cun* with a local sensation of soreness and distension. For trigeminal neuralgia, the tip of the needle should be tilted obliquely towards the latero-superior aspect into the infra-orbital foramen with a sensation of numbness like electric shock radiating to the upper lip. Deep insertion of needle is not allowed because it will cause injury to the eyeball. Moxibustion is contraindicated.

Nose-Juliao (St. 3)

Location: Directly below Sibai (St. 2) 0.8 *cun* by the border of alae nasi.

Function: Dispersing wind, activating blood circulation of the channels.

Indications: Deviation of the mouth, epistaxis, toothache.

Points combination: Nose-Juliao (St. 3) combined with Jiache (St. 6), Yifeng (S.J. 17) and Hegu (L.I. 4): deviated mouth and eye; with Xiaguan (St. 7), Chize (Lu. 5) and Xiangu (St. 43):

pain and swelling of cheeks; with Yifeng (S.J. 17), Dicang (St. 4) and Sibai (St. 2): twitching of facial muscle.

Method: Puncture perpendicularly 0.3-0.5 *cun* with a sensation of soreness and distension. Moxibustion is applicable.

Dicang (St. 4)

Location: 0.5 *cun* lateral to the corner of the mouth.

Function: Dispersing wind, regulating the circulation of Qi and removing obstruction from channels.

Indications: Deviation of the mouth and eyes, excessive salivation, facial paralysis, spasm of the facial nerve, trigeminal neuralgia.

Points combination: Dicang (St. 4) combined with Jiache (St. 6): deviated mouth and eye; with Chengqi (St. 1): salivation; with Yuyao (Extra) and Sibai (St. 2): trigeminal neuralgia.

Method: Transverse insertion towards the Jiache (St. 6).

Jiache (St. 6)

Location: In the masseter muscle, at the prominence of the muscle when the teeth are clenched.

Function: Removing obstruction of channels, dispersing wind, and clearing heat.

Indications: Lower toothache, temporomandibular arthritis, facial paralysis, mumps.

Points combination: Jiache (St. 6) combined with Dicang (St. 4) and Yifeng (S.J. 17): deviated mouth and eye, salivation; with Renzhong (Du 26) and Hegu (L.I. 4): trismus due to wind-stroke; with Hegu (L.I. 4) and Neiting (St. 44): toothache; with Yifeng (S.J. 17) and Quchi (L.I. 11): parotitis.

Method: Straight or slanted insertion towards the corner of the mouth 0.5 to 1 *cun*.

Xiaguan (St. 7)

Location: At the front of the ear and at the lower border of the zygomatic arch. With the mouth closed, in the hollow formed between the zygomatic arch and the mandibular.

Function: Dispersing wind, clearing heat, opening lockjaws and stopping pain.

Indications: Upper toothache, facial paralysis, temporomandibular arthritis, pain in the heel, motor impairment of the jaw.

Points combination: Xiaguan (St. 7) combined with Hegu (L.I. 4): lower mandibular arthritis; with Jiache (St. 6): spasm of masseter muscle; with Daying (St. 5) and Taiyang (Extra): trigeminal neuralgia; with Waiguan (S.J. 5) and Tinggong (S.I. 19): ear diseases; with Sanjian (L.I. 3) and Xiangu (St. 43): toothache.

Method: Straight insertion 0.5 to 1 *cun* with mouth closed.

Tianshu (St. 25, Front-Mu Point of the large intestine)

Location: Two *cun* lateral to the navel.

Function: Adjusting the functions of the stomach and intestines, regulating Qi circulation and dissolving damp.

Indications: Abdominal distension, diarrhea, dysentery, constipation, intestinal paralysis, leukorrhea, urethra infection, vomiting.

Points combination: Tianshu (St. 25) combined with Zhongwan (Ren 12), Guanyuan (Ren 4), Hegu (L.I. 4) and Zusanli (St. 36): abdominal pain and diarrhea; with Shangjuxu (St. 37) and Guanyuan (Ren 4): appendicitis; with Guanyuan (Ren 4) and Diji (Sp. 8): excessive leukorrhea; with Sanyinjiao (Sp. 6) and Ciliao (U.B. 32): premenstrual pain; with Jingmen (G.B. 25) and Zusanli (St. 36): lower abdominal pain.

Method: Straight insertion, 1-2 *cun*. Needling sensation may extend throughout the side of the abdomen.

Qichong (St. 30)

Location: 5 *cun* below umbilicus, 2 *cun* lateral to the Ren Channel, at the level with Qugu (Ren 2).

Function: Relaxing tendons, harmonizing Ying (nutrient) Qi, removing the obstruction of Qi circulation and regulating the function of the uterus.

Indications: Hernia, irregular menstruation, infertility, impotence, swelling and pain of penis, fullness and distension of the abdomen and obstetrical disorders.

Points combination: Qichong (St. 30) combined with Guanyuan (Ren 4): pain of penis; with Zhangmen (Liv. 13): restlessness of sleep; with Ququan (Liv. 8) and Taichong (Liv. 3): hernia; with Zhongji (Ren 3) and Sanyinjiao (Sp. 6): infection of urinary system; with Baohuang (U.B. 53) and Lougu (Sp. 7): irregular menstruation.

Method: Puncture perpendicularly 0.5-1 *cun* with a local sensation of heaviness and distension. Puncture obliquely towards the external genital region 1-2 *cun* with a local sensation of soreness and distension for disorders of urinogenital system. Avoid the artery during puncturing. Moxibustion is not applicable.

Zusanli (St. 36, He-Sea Point)

Location: Three *cun* below the knee, approximately 1 finger width lateral to the tibia (*Fig.* 2-9).

Function: Building up the spleen and stomach, removing the obstruction of channels, regulating Qi circulation of channels and collaterals.

Indications: Abdominal pain and distension, constipation, diarrhea, vomiting, indigestion, anemia, weakness, pain in lower limb, paralysis, insomnia, eye diseases, pain in knee and shoulder.

Points combination: Zusanli (St. 36) combined with Zhongwan (Ren 12), Tianshu (St. 25), Neiguan (P. 6) and Gongsun (Sp. 4): disorders of the intestines and stomach; with Baihui (Du 20), Renzhong (Du 26) and Taichong (Liv. 3): dizziness, syncope; with Huantiao (G.B. 30), Weizhong (U.B. 40), Yanglingquan (G.B. 34) and Sanyinjiao (Sp. 6): atrophy and paralysis of lower limbs; with Guanyuan (Ren 4): to tonify the body and prevent wind-stroke; with Shuidao (St. 28) and Shenshu (U.B. 23): edema and dysuria; with Rugen (St. 18) and Diwuhui (G.B. 42): mastitis; with Liangqiu (St. 34) and Dubi (St. 35): swelling and pain of the knees; with Xiajuxu (St. 39), Yanglingquan (G.B. 34) and Neiguan (P. 6): pancreatitis; with Zhongfeng (Liv. 4), Qiuxu (G.B. 40), Qimen (Liv. 14) and Riyue (G.B. 24): disorders of the liver and gall bladder; with Quchi (L.I. 11) and Hegu (L.I. 4): low fever and urticaria.

Method: Straight insertion, 1-1.5 *cun*. Needling sensation may extend towards the foot, or up towards the knee joint. Moxibustion may be applied for 5-10 minutes.

Shangjuxu (St. 37, Lower He-Sea Point of the large intestine)

Location: 3 *cun* directly below Zusanli (St. 36).

Function: Regulating the spleen, harmonizing the stomach, removing the obstruction of the Fu organs and the channels, and relieving Wei syndromes at acute stage.

Indications: Borborygmus, abdominal pain, diarrhea, constipation, dysentery, appendicitis, Wei and Bi syndromes of the lower limb.

Points combination: Shangjuxu (St. 37) combined with Tianshu (St. 25) and Quchi (L.I. 11): dysentery and enteritis; with Fujie (Sp. 14): constipation; with Jiexi (St. 41): foot drop; with Qihai (Ren 6): abdominal distension and pain; with Huantiao (G.B. 30) and Sanyinjiao (Sp. 6): paralysis of lower limbs.

Method: Puncture perpendicularly 2-3 *cun* with a sensation of numbness like electric shock radiating down to the foot. This sensation should be certainly obtained for treating foot drop and spasm of lower leg. Moxibustion is applicable.

Tiaokou (St. 38)

Location: Five *cun* below Zusanli (St. 36) (See *Fig.* 2-9).

Function: Relaxing the tendons, activating the blood circulation and stopping pain.

Indications: Numbness, soreness and pain in knee, spasm, swelling of the instep, paralysis of the leg, shoulder pain.

Points combination: Tiaokou (St. 38) combined with Xuanzhong (Juegu, G.B. 39) and Chongyang (St. 42): pain and swelling in the front of tibia; with Zusanli (St. 36), Chengshan (U.B. 57) and Chengjin (U.B. 56): pain, swelling, redness and motor impairment of the knee and thigh, and cramps of the leg; puncturing from Tiaokou (St. 38) towards Chengshan (U.B. 57): frozen shoulder and shoulder pain; with Zhiyin (U.B. 67), Rangu (K. 2) and Yongquan (K. 1): feverish sensation of the sole of foot.

Method: Puncture perpendicularly 1.5-2.5 *cun* with a sensation of soreness and distension in the front of the leg, radiating down to the dorsum of foot. Moxibustion is applicable.

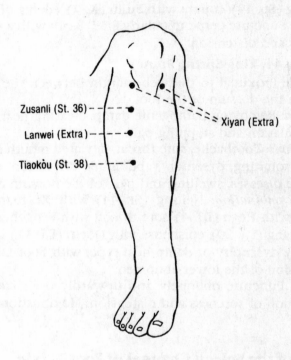

Zusanli (St. 36)
Lanwei (Extra)
Tiaokòu (St. 38)
Xiyan (Extra)

Fig. 2-9.

Fenglong (St. 40, Luo-Connecting Point)

Location: On the lower leg, 8 *cun* above the lateral malleolus of the ankle between the tibialis and peroneus bones.

Function: Harmonizing the stomach, dissolving phlegm and easing the mind.

Indications: Asthma, cough, abundant mucus, vertigo, headache, congested and sore throat, lower limb pain.

Points combination: Fenglong (St. 40) combined with Fujie (Sp. 14) and Fushe (Sp. 13): constipation; with Fengchi (G.B. 20) and Shenmen (H. 7): insomnia; with Tiantu (Ren 22), Fengmen (U.B. 12), Zhongwan (Ren 12), Chize (Lu. 5) and Zusanli (St. 36): asthma with excessive sputum; with Feishu (U.B. 13) and

Xiongxiang (Sp. 19): cough; with Fuliu (K. 7): edema of limbs.

Method: Puncture perpendicularly 0.5-0.8 *cun* with a sensation of soreness and distension.

Neiting (St. 44, Ying-Spring Point)

Location: Proximal to the web margin between the 2nd and 3rd toes on the dorsum of the foot.

Function: Removing pathogenic damp, clearing heat, regulating Qi circulation and stopping pain.

Indications: Toothache, sore throat, deviated mouth and eyes, gastralgia, vomiting, dysentery, abdominal distension, constipation, febrile diseases, swelling and pain of the dorsum of foot.

Points combination: Neiting (St. 44) with Xiaguan (St. 7): toothache; with Hegu (L.I. 4): sore throat; with Fengchi (G.B. 20) and Yingxiang (L.I. 20): epistaxis; with Quchi (L.I. 11) and Tianshu (St. 25): dysentery of damp-heat type; with Foot-Linqi (G.B. 41): distension of the lower abdomen.

Method: Puncture obliquely and upwardly 0.5-1 *cun* with a local sensation of soreness and distension. Moxibustion is applicable.

4. Points of the Spleen Channel of Foot-Taiyin

Dadu (Sp. 2, Ying-Spring Point)

Location: On the medial side of the big toe, anterior and inferior to the first metatarsodigital joint, at the junction of the red and white skin.

Function: Building up the spleen, harmonizing the stomach, clearing heat and relieving exterior syndromes.

Indications: Abdominal distension, stomachache, fever without sweating, vomiting, fullness of chest and anorexia.

Points combination: Dadu (Sp. 2) combined with Neiguan (P. 6) and Zusanli (St. 36): indigestion; with Taibai (Sp. 3): severe diarrhea and abdominal distension; with Jingqu (Lu. 8): fever without sweating; with Zhongchong (P. 9), Guanchong (S.J. 1), Hegu (L.I. 4) and Taichong (Liv. 3): coldness of four extremities.

Method: Puncture obliquely 0.5-0.8 *cun* with local sensation of soreness. Moxibustion is applicable.

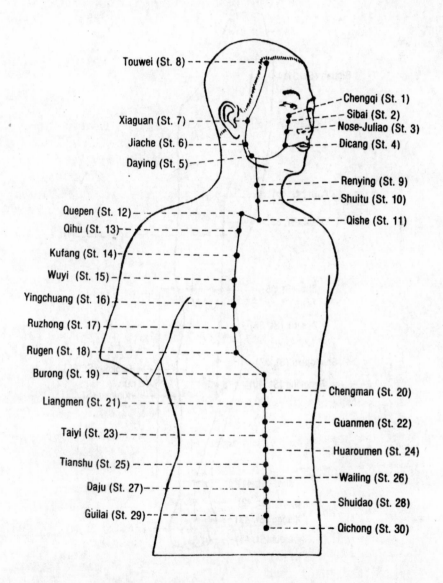

Fig. 2-10a. The Stomach Channel of Foot-Yangming.

41

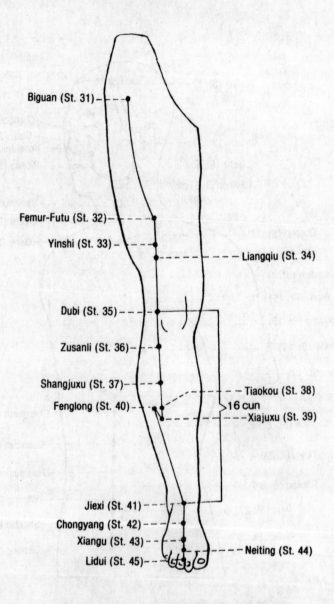

Fig. 2-10b. The Stomach Channel of Foot-Yangming.

Gongsun (Sp. 4, Luo-Connecting Point, one of the eight confluent points, communicating with Chong Channel)

Location: On the medial aspect of the foot at anterior, inferior margin of the 1st metatarsus, 1 *cun* behind the joint of the big toe.

Function: Building up the spleen, regulating Qi circulation in the channels, dissolving damp and harmonizing the stomach.

Indications: Vomiting, distension and fullness of the abdomen, indigestion, dysmenorrhea.

Points combination: Gongsun (Sp. 4) combined with Neiguan (P. 6): disorders of the stomach, heart and chest; with Baihui (Du 20), Renzhong (Du 26), Hegu (L.I. 4) and Taichong (Liv. 3): epilepsy, mental depression and mania; with Chongyang (St. 42) and Zusanli (St. 36): beriberi, edema; with Zusanli (St. 36), Neiting (St. 44) and Neiguan (P. 6): bleeding of digestive tract.

Method: Straight insertion, 1-1.5 *cun*. Moxibustion may be applied for 5-10 minutes.

Shangqiu (Sp. 5, Jing-River Point)

Location: In the depression anterior and inferior to the medial malleolus, midway between the tuberosity of the navicular bone and the tip of the medial malleolus.

Function: Strengthening the spleen and removing dampness.

Indications: Abdominal distension, borborygmus, diarrhea, constipation, indigestion, sighing, stiffness of the tongue, dysphasia, pain of ankle joint, hernia, infantile convulsion.

Points combination: Shangqiu (Sp. 5) combined with Neiguan (P. 6): vomiting and sighing; with Lianquan (Ren 23) and Fengchi (G.B. 20): stiffness of the tongue and dysphasia; with Diwuhui (G.B. 42), Foot-Qiaoyin (G.B. 44) and Tiaokou (St. 38): foot pain, pain and swelling of ankle joint; with Tianshu (St. 25), Guanyuan (Ren 4) and Zusanli (St. 36): diarrhea; with Quchi (L.I. 11) and Feishu (U.B. 13): whooping cough; with Chengshan (U.B. 57): hemorrhoids and constipation; with Sanyinjiao (Sp. 6) and Guilai (St. 29): infertility in women; with Pishu (U.B. 20), Weishu (U.B.

21) and Zhongwan (Ren 12): infantile convulsion.

Method: Puncture perpendicularly 0.5-0.8 *cun*. Puncture horizontally 1-1.5 *cun* towards Jiexi (St. 41) with a local sensation of soreness, distension and heaviness around ankle joint. Moxibustion is applicable.

Sanyinjiao (Sp. 6)

Location: At the posterior margin of the tibia, 3 *cun* above the medial malleolus of the ankle (*Fig.* 2-11).

Function: Reinforcing the spleen and stomach, promoting transportation and transformation, removing the obstruction from the channels, regulating the circulation of Qi and blood, benefiting the liver and kidney, and pacifying the reversed Qi.

Indications: Irregular menstruation, uterine bleeding, dysmenorrhea, leukorrhea, pain in vagina, neurasthenia, insomnia, impotence, seminal emission, nocturnal emission, indigestion, diarrhea, atrophy of the lower limb, hemiplegia, hemorrhoids, colic.

Points combination: Sanyinjiao (Sp. 6) combined with Guilai (St. 29) and Taichong (Liv. 3): hernia; with Xuehai (Sp. 10), Guanyuan (Ren 4) and Zhigou (S.J. 6): spermatorrhea and excessive leukorrhea; with Qihai (Ren 6) and Zhongji (Ren 3): enuresis; with Shenmen (H. 7): insomnia; with Zusanli (St. 36) and Tianshu (St. 25): abdominal distension and pain; with Neiguan (P. 6): hysteria; with Shenshu (U.B. 23) and Hegu (L.I. 4): transverse lie; with Shuifen (Ren 9) and Fenglong (St. 40): edema; with Renzhong (Du 26) and Neiguan (P. 6): wind-stroke; with Baihui (Du 20) and Quchi (L.I. 11): hypertension; with Weizhong (U.B. 40) and Yanglingquan (G.B. 34): Wei and Bi Syndromes of lower limbs.

Method: Straight insertion, 1-3 *cun*, needling sensation may extend downward to the foot and up along the medial aspect of the thigh.

Yinlingquan (Sp. 9, He-Sea Point)

Location: In the depression at the inferior margin of the medial condyle of the tibia (See *Fig.* 2-11).

Function: Building up the spleen, dissolving damp, removing

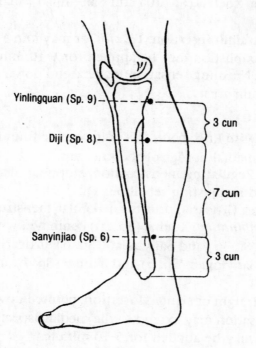

Fig. 2-11.

the obstruction of the Sanjiao.

Indications: Distension of the abdomen, diarrhea, edema, pain in knee, difficult urination, insufficient urine, incontinence of urine, nocturnal emission, impotence, seminal emission, pain of the lower back and leg, women's diseases.

Points combination: Yinlingquan (Sp. 9) combined with Shuifen (Ren 9), Zhongji (Ren 3), Zusanli (St. 36) and Sanyinjiao (Sp. 6): retention of urine and ascites; with Chengshan (U.B. 57), Jiexi (St. 41) and Taibai (Sp. 3): cholera; with Yanglingquan (G.B. 34) and Heding (Extra): knee arthritis; with Shaofu (H. 8) and Lieque (Lu. 7): pain of penis; with Yinbai (Sp. 1): feverish sensation in the chest, acute diarrhea and abdominal pain; with Guanyuan (Ren 4) and Yanglingquan (G.B. 34): incontinence of urine and enuresis; with Xuehai (Sp. 10) and Sanyinjiao (Sp. 6): edema of lower limbs.

Method: Straight insertion, 1-2 *cun*, or may join Yanglingquan (G.B. 34). Moxibustion may be applied for 5-10 minutes.

Sensation: Needling sensation may extend down to foot or up to the perineum area.

Xuehai (Sp. 10)

Location: With knee bent, this point can be found 2 *cun* above the superior medial border of the kneecap.

Function: Regulating menstruation, stopping bleeding, expelling wind and readjusting rebellious Qi.

Indications: Urticaria, pruritus, irregular menstruation.

Points combination: Xuehai (Sp. 10) combined with Quchi (L.I. 11), Zusanli (St. 36) and Sanyinjiao (Sp. 6): urticaria; with Shuiquan (K. 5), Sanyinjiao (Sp. 6) and Yinbai (Sp. 1): uterine bleeding.

Method: Straight or slanted insertion, pointed upward, 1-3 *cun*. Needling sensation may extend to the medial aspect of the thigh. Moxibustion may be applied for 5-10 minutes.

Fujie (Sp. 14)

Location: 4 *cun* lateral to the Ren Channel, 1.3 *cun* below Daheng (Sp. 15).

Function: Regulating the circulation of Qi and descending reversive flowing Qi.

Indications: Abdominal pain, dysentery, constipation and hernia.

Points combination: Fujie (Sp. 14) combined with moxibustion on Shenque (Ren 8): abdominal pain around umbilicus; with Taichong (Liv. 3): reversive flowing Qi causes heart problems; with Shangjuxu (St. 37) and Tianshu (St. 25): abdominal pain and diarrhea; with Yanglingquan (G.B. 34): hypochondriac and costal pain; with Fushe (Sp. 13) and Shangjuxu (St. 37): constipation.

Method: Puncture perpendicularly 1.5 *cun* with local sensation of numbness and distension. Moxibustion is applicable.

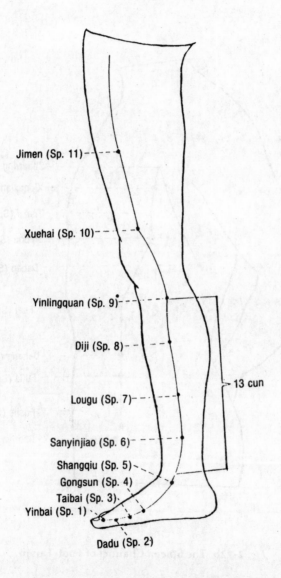

Jimen (Sp. 11)

Xuehai (Sp. 10)

Yinlingquan (Sp. 9)

Diji (Sp. 8)

13 cun

Lougu (Sp. 7)

Sanyinjiao (Sp. 6)

Shangqiu (Sp. 5)

Gongsun (Sp. 4)

Taibai (Sp. 3)

Yinbai (Sp. 1)

Dadu (Sp. 2)

Fig. 2-12a. The Spleen Channel of Foot-Taiyin.

47

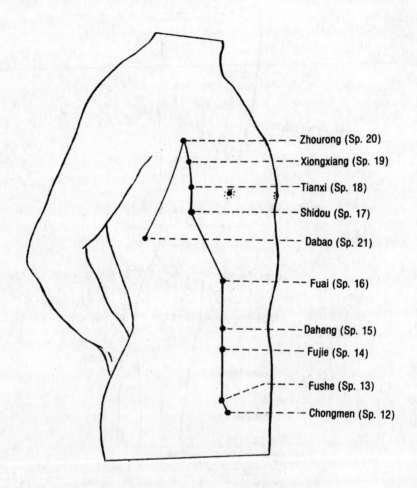

Fig. 2-12b. The Spleen Channel of Foot-Taiyin.

5. Points of the Heart Channel of Hand-Shaoyin

Jiquan (H. 1)

Location: In the center of the axillary on the medial side of the axillary artery.

Function: Tranquilizing the heart, stopping pain, removing obstruction of the channel and activating blood circulation.

Indications: Chest pain, paralysis of the upper limb, shoulder pain with motor impairment and the injury of plexus brachialis.

Points combination: Jiquan (H. 1) combined with Shenfeng (K. 23), Shanzhong (Ren 17) and Xiabai (Lu. 4): heart pain and stiffness of the chest; with Lingxu (K. 24), Diwuhui (G.B. 42) and Yuzhong (K. 26): mental depression; with Zhigou (S.J. 6) and Taichong (Liv. 3): hypochondriac pain; with Neiguan (P. 6): paralysis of the upper limb; with Jianyu (L.I. 15) and Jianzhen (S.I. 9): frozen shoulder; with Quepen (St. 12), Quze (P. 3) and Chize (Lu. 5): injury of plexus brachialis.

Method: Puncture perpendicularly 1-1.5 *cun* with a sensation of soreness and numbness which may radiate to the forearm and the tips of fingers. Moxibustion is applicable. In treating paralysis of the upper limb and the injury of nervous plexus brachialis, the sensation of numbness like electric shock should radiate to the upper arm. Retention of the needle is unnecessary.

Qingling (H. 2)

Location: 3 *cun* above Shaohai (H. 3) on the line connecting Jiquan (H. 1) and Shaohai (H. 3), in the groove medial to m. biceps brachii.

Function: Relaxing the tendons, relieving Wei syndromes, removing the obstruction from the channels and stopping pain.

Indications: Weakness of elbow and wrist, inability of flexion and extension, paralysis, difficulty of raising up shoulder and arm, injury of ulna and median nerves.

Points combination: Qingling (H. 2) combined with Xinshu (U.B. 15) and Ximen (P. 4): angina pectoris; with Jianyu (L.I. 15) and Quchi (L.I. 11): pain of shoulder and arm; with Jiquan (H. 1), Tianding (L.I. 17), Neiguan (P. 6), Hegu (L.I. 4) and Chize (Lu. 5):

injury of nervous plexus brachialis; with Ximen (P. 4) and Neiguan (P. 6): pain of median nerve.

Method: Puncture perpendicularly 0.5-1 *cun* with a local sensation of soreness and distension which may radiate to the
forearm. Moxibustion is applicable. The artery should be avoided
while inserting the needle. Even lifting and thrusting movements
of the needle can be employed until the sensation radiates along
the forearm to the fingers and there is a slight flexion of the
fingers.

Shaohai (H. 3, He-Sea Point)

Location: With the arm bent at the elbow, this point can be
found in the depression between the end of the transverse crease
on the ulnar side of the elbow and the medial condyle of the
humerus.

Function: Benefiting the heart, easing the mind, removing the
obstruction from channels and regulating the circulation of Qi.

Indications: Pain in the elbow, hand tremors, insomnia, mental disorders.

Points combination: Shaohai (H. 3) combined with Chize (Lu.
5) and Neiguan (P. 6): paralysis of upper limbs; with Hegu (L.I. 4)
and Houxi (S.I. 3): tremor of hands; with Hegu (L.I. 4) and Neiting
(St. 44): toothache of Xu and Shi types; with Neiguan (P. 6),
Shanzhong (Ren 17), and Shenfeng (K. 23): pain of the heart and
chest.

Method: Straight insertion 0.5-1 *cun*.

Sensation: Local soreness and distension, or sensation extending towards the forearm.

Tongli (H. 5, Luo-Connecting Point)

Location: One *cun* above the transverse crease of the wrist.

Function: Clearing the heart, easing the mind, relieving symptoms of tongue and harmonizing the Ying (nutrient) Qi.

Indications: Palpitation, aphasia with stiffness of the tongue.

Points combination: Tongli (H. 5) combined with Neiguan (P.
6) and Xinshu (U.B. 15): arrhythmia and angina pectoris; with
Jinjin/Yuye (Extra): aphasia caused by stiffness of the tongue;

with Shenmen (H. 7) and Taichong (Liv. 3): dementia; with
Xingjian (Liv. 2) and Sanyinjiao (Sp. 6): excessive menstruation;
with Dazhong (K. 4): listlessness and hypersomnia, and Tongziliao (G.B. 1): blurred vision and night-blindness; with Tongziliao
(G.B. 1): spasm of orbicular muscle of eye; with Fengchi (G.B. 20)
and Hegu (L.I. 4): retrobulbar neuritis and optic atrophy; with
Jingming (U.B. 1), Taiyang (Extra) and Taichong (Liv. 3): glau-
coma.

Method: Puncture perpendicularly 0.5-1 *cun* along the infra-
orbital ridge with a fine needle. Be sure there is no lifting,
thrusting or rotating of the needle in wide amplitude.

Sensation: The acupuncture sensation is local soreness and
distention, sometimes with tears. Soon after withdrawal of the
needle, press the needle hole for a few minutes in order to avoid
bleeding. Moxibustion is contraindicated.

Shenmen (H. 7, Shu-Stream and Yuan-Source Point)

Location: This point can be found in the small hollow on the
ulnar aspect at the end of the transverse crease of the wrist.

Function: Clearing fire from the heart, harmonizing Ying
(nutrient) Qi and easing the mind.

Indications: Insomnia, absent-mindedness, angina pectoris,
psychosis.

Points combination: Shenmen (H. 7) combined with Fengchi
(G.B. 20), Baihui (Du 20) and Sanyinjiao (Sp. 6): neurasthenia;
with Neiguan (P. 6), Yintang (Extra) and Zusanli (St. 36): hysteria,
palpitation and insomnia; with Shaoshang (Lu. 11), Yongquan (K.
1) and Xinshu (U.B. 15): dementia; with Neiguan (P. 6), Xinshu
(U.B. 15) and Shanzhong (Ren 17): angina pectoris.

Method: Straight insertion, 3 *cun*.

Shaofu (H. 8, Ying-Spring Point)

Location: With the hand supine and the fingers cupped in a
half fist, this point can be found on the palm just below the tip
of the little finger.

Function: Clearing pathogenic factors from the heart, easing
the mind, regulating the function of Qi and dissolving damp.

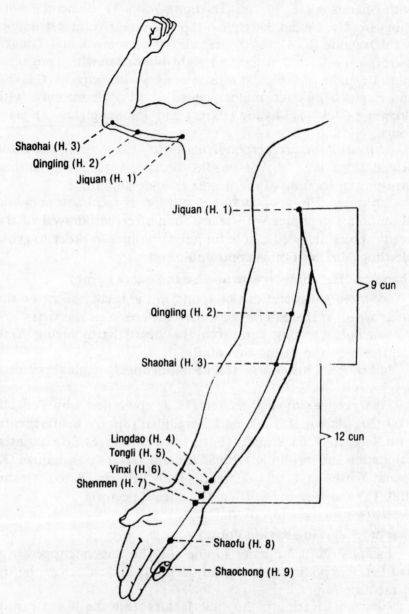

Fig. 2-13. The Heart Channel of Hand-Shaoyin.

Shaohai (H. 3)
Qingling (H. 2)
Jiquan (H. 1)

Jiquan (H. 1)

9 cun

Qingling (H. 2)

Shaohai (H. 3)

12 cun

Lingdao (H. 4)
Tongli (H. 5)
Yinxi (H. 6)
Shenmen (H. 7)

Shaofu (H. 8)

Shaochong (H. 9)

Indications: Palpitation, pain in the chest.

Points combinations: Shaofu (H. 8) combined with Neiguan (P. 6), Sanyinjiao (Sp. 6) and Shenfeng (K. 23): angina pectoris; with Lingdao (H. 4): spasm of the little finger; with Ligou (Liv. 5) and Yinlingquan (Sp. 9): pruritus vulvae; with Quchi (L.I. 11) and Daling (P. 7): hotness in the palm.

Method: Puncture perpendicularly 0.3-0.5 *cun*. With a local senation of aching, soreness and distension, and slight moving of the little and ring fingers. Moxibustion is applicable.

Shaochong (H. 9, Jing-Well Point)

Location: On the radial aspect of the little finger, 0.1 *cun* posterior to the corner of the nail.

Function: Resuscitating the mind, opening the orifices, reducing heat.

Indications: Heart pain, palpitation, windstroke, coma, irritability, febrile diseases.

Points combination: Shaochong (H. 9) plus Renzhong (Du 26), Hegu (L.I. 4) and Zusanli (St. 36): windstroke, sunstroke, shock and coma; plus other Jing-Well Points: fever; plus Daling (P. 7): palpitation, irritability and fullness of the chest.

Method: Puncture perpendicularly 0.1 *cun* with a local sensation of aching. Or pricking with three-edged needle to cause bleeding. Moxibustion is applicable.

6. Points of the Small Intestine Channel of Hand-Taiyang

Shaoze (S.I. 1, Jing-Well Point)

Location: On the ulnar aspect of the little finger, about 0.1 *cun* outside the corner of the cuticle (*Fig.* 2-14).

Function: Promoting resuscitation and mental clearness, and relieving swelling and pain, and removing letax.

Indications: Fainting, neuralgic headache, deafness, mastitis, insufficient lactation, membrane on the eye.

Points combination: Shaoze (S.I. 1) combined with Fengchi (G.B. 20): stiffness of neck and pain of occipital region; with

Tinggong (S.I. 19) and Yifeng (S.J. 17): ringing in the ears and deafness; with Rugen (St. 18), Shanzhong (Ren 17) and Hegu (L.I. 4): mastitis and deficient lactation.

Method: Puncture perpendicularly 0.1 *cun* with a sensation of local aching, or pricking with three-edged needle to let blood out. Moxibustion is applicable.

Houxi (S.I. 3, Shu-Stream Point, Confluent Point of Eight Extra Channels, connecting with Du Channel)

Location: When the hand is clenched in a fist, this point can be found behind and lateral to the head of the 5th metacarpus, at the top of the transverse crease formed by the clenched fist (See *Fig.* 2-14).

Function: Clearing heat, tranquilizing the heart, expelling wind and removing the obstruction from the channels.

Indications: Stiff neck, pain in lower back and rib, seizure, facial paralysis.

Points combination: Houxi (S.I. 3) combined with Shenmai (U.B. 62) as one pair of Confluent Points: headache, stiffness of neck, redness, swelling and pain of eyes, and low back pain; with Dazhui (Du 14) and Jianshi (P. 5): tertiary fever; with Fengfu (Du 16): pain of the nape of neck and headache; with Fengchi (G.B. 20) and Dazhui (Du 14): fever of common cold; with Jianyu (L.I. 15) and Tianzong (S.I. 11): pain of back and shoulder.

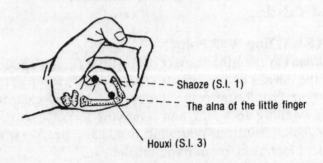

Shaoze (S.I. 1)

The alna of the little finger

Houxi (S.I. 3)

Fig. 2-14.

Method: Straight insertion, 0.5-1 *cun*. For stiff neck and lower back sprain, join to Hegu (L.I. 4).

Yanglao (S.I. 6, Xi-Cleft Point)

Location: With the palm facing the chest, this point can be found in a seam slightly above the head of the ulna on its radial side.

Function: Relaxing tendons, removing obstruction from channels, brightening eyes and dispersing wind.

Indications: Stiff neck, pain in chest, distension in the chest, pain in back, shoulder and arm.

Points combination: Yanglao (S.I. 6) combined with Tianzhu (U.B. 10): blurred vision; with Fengchi (G.B. 20): stiffness of neck; with Neiguan (P. 6) and Geshu (U.B. 17): hiccough; with Quchi (L.I. 11) and Jianyu (L.I. 15): pain of wrist, elbow and shoulder.

Method: Slanted insertion, with the needle pointed towards Neiguan (P. 6), 1-1.5 *cun*.

Sensation: Local needling sensation may extend to the shoulder.

Jianzhen (S.I. 9)

Location: When the arm is abducted, it is 1 *cun* above the posterior end of the axillary fold.

Function: Dispelling the pathogenic wind, activating the blood circulation, removing the obstruction of channels.

Indications: Pain of shoulder and arm with motor impairment, tinnitus, and scrofula.

Points combination: Jianzhen (S.I. 9) combined with Jianyu (L.I. 15), Jianliao (S.J. 14): shoulder joint pain; with Tianzong (S.I. 11) and Bingfeng (S.I. 12): scapular and back pain; with Naoshu (S.I. 10), Houxi (S.I. 3) and Jianyu (L.I. 15): arm pain with motor impairment; with Jianyu (L.I. 15): injury of axillary nerve.

Method: Puncture perpendicularly 1-1.5 *cun* with a local sensation of soreness and distension. Moxibustion is applicable. Puncture obliquely and superiorly 2-2.5 *cun* with a sensation of soreness, distension and numbness radiating towards the whole shoulder and the scapular region for pain and motor impairment of the shoulder and injury of axillary nerve. Puncture obliquely and superior laterally 2-2.5 *cun* with the sensation of electric shock radiating towards the posterior aspect of the upper arm and the tips of fingers.

Naoshu (S.I. 10)

Location: With the arm hanging down, the point can be found directly above the armpit, below the big bone (See *Fig.* 2-5 on page 29).

Function: Relaxing the tendons, promoting the blood circulation in vessels, dispelling pathogenic wind and stopping pain.

Indications: Pain in shoulder.

Points combination: Ñaoshu (S.I. 10) combined with Jianyu (L.I. 15), Jianliao (S.J. 14) and Yanglao (S.I. 6): pain of shoulder and arm with motor impairment; with Tiantu (Ren 22) and Fengchi (G.B. 20): pain of shoulder referring to the upper back; with Houxi (S.I. 3) and Jianjing (G.B. 21): shoulder pain.

Method: Puncture obliquely towards the anterior-interior aspect of the point for 1.5-2 *cun* with a local sensation of soreness and distension, sometimes radiating to the shoulder region. Moxibustion is advisable.

Tianzong (S.I. 11)

Location: In the center of the infrascapular fossa.

Function: Relaxing the tendons, dispelling pathogenic wind, promoting the circulation of Qi and releasing the chest.

Indications: Scapular pain, asthma and mastitis.

Points combination: Tianzong (S.I. 11) combined with Jianyu (L.I. 15), Jianliao (S.J. 14), Quchi (L.I. 11) and Yanglao (S.I. 6): peripheral inflammation of shoulder joint; with Shanzhong (Ren 17), Rugen (St. 18) and Shaoze (S.I. 1): mastitis and deficient lacrimation; with Feishu (U.B. 13): cough and asthma.

Method: Puncture perpendicularly 0.3-0.5 *cun*, or puncture obliquely towards four directions 0.5-1.5 *cun* with a local sensation of soreness and distension. Moxibustion is advisable.

Bingfeng (S.I. 12)

Location: In the center of suprascapular fossa, directly above

Tianzong (S.I. 11). When the arm is lifted, it is in the depression.

Function: Relaxing the tendons and removing the obstruction of channels.

Indications: Pain in the scapular region, numbness of the upper arm and stiffness of the neck.

Points combination: Bingfeng (S.I. 12) combined with Yunmen (Lu. 2): shoulder pain with motor impairment; with Tianrong (S.I. 17): wondering pain of the shoulder region; with Fengchi (G.B. 20) and Tianzhu (U.B. 10): stiffness of the neck; with Tianzong (S.I. 11) and Houxi (S.I. 3): scapular and back pain.

Method: Puncture perpendicularly 0.5-0.8 *cun* or puncture obliquely one *cun* with a local sensation of soreness and distension. Moxibustion is applicable.

Tianrong (S.I. 17)

Location: Posterior to the angle of mandible, on the anterior border of m. sterno-cleidomastoideus.

Function: Removing obstruction of channels, regulating the circulation of Qi, relieving sore throat.

Indications: Ringing in the ears, deafness, sore throat.

Points combination: Tianrong (S.I. 17) with Hegu (L.I. 4) and Shaoshang (Lu. 11): tonsillitis and pharyngitis; with Hegu (L.I. 4): mumps.

Method: Puncture perpendicularly 1-1.5 *cun* deep to the root of tongue with a local sensation of soreness and distension, then spreading to the root of tongue or to the throat. Moxibustion is advisable. The point is near the external carotic artery. This artery should be avoided while puncturing. Lifting and thrusting of the needle in wide amplitude is not appropriate.

Tinggong (S.I. 19)

Location: In the depression anterior to the middle of the tragus of the ear when the mouth is open (*Fig.* 2-15).

Function: Improving the hearing, opening the orifices, removing obstruction from vessels and stopping pain.

Indications: Deafness, ringing in the ears, deaf-mutism, parotitis, inflammation of the ear canal.

Points combination: Tinggong (S.I. 19) combined with Tinghui

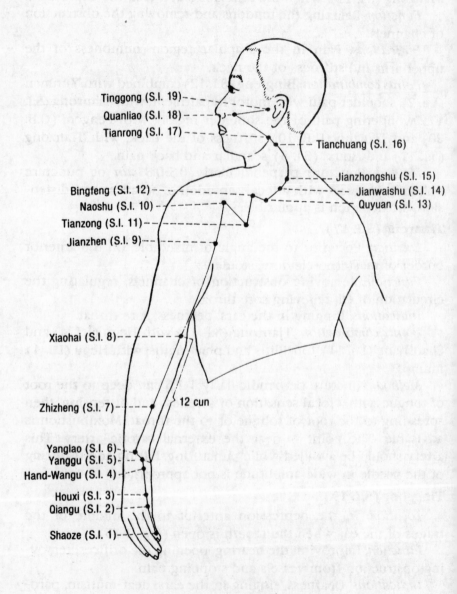

Tinggong (S.I. 19)

Quanliao (S.I. 18)

Tianrong (S.I. 17)

Tianchuang (S.I. 16)

Jianzhongshu (S.I. 15)

Bingfeng (S.I. 12)

Jianwaishu (S.I. 14)

Naoshu (S.I. 10)

Quyuan (S.I. 13)

Tianzong (S.I. 11)

Jianzhen (S.I. 9)

Xiaohai (S.I. 8)

Zhizheng (S.I. 7)

12 cun

Yanglao (S.I. 6)

Yanggu (S.I. 5)

Hand-Wangu (S.I. 4)

Houxi (S.I. 3)

Qiangu (S.I. 2)

Shaoze (S.I. 1)

Fig. 2-15. The Small Intestine Channel of Hand-Taiyang.

(G.B. 2), Head-Qiaoyin (G.B. 11), Hand-Zhongzhu (S.J. 3) and Yangfu (G.B. 38): tinnitus and deafness; with Xiaguan (St. 7) and Hegu (L.I. 4): lower mandibular arthritis; with Yifeng (S.J. 17) and Waiguan (S.J. 5): otitis media.

Method: Straight insertion with mouth open.

Sensation: Local distension when inserted 1 *cun*, possibly extending throughout the whole ear, sometimes a sensation expanding outwards from inside the ear, and tingling at the side of the head.

7. Points of the Urinary Bladder Channel of Foot-Taiyang

Jingming (U.B. 1)

Location: 0.1 *cun* above the inner canthus of the eye (See *Fig.* 2-8 on page 34).

Function: Dispersing wind, reducing fire, nourishing Yin and brightening vision.

Indications: Excessive tearing on exposure to wind, night blindness, neuritis of the optic nerve, optic neuritis, atrophy of the optic nerve, cataract.

Points combination: Jingming (U.B. 1) combined with Ganshu (U.B. 18), Taiyang (Extra), Jiaosun (S.J. 20) and Hegu (L.I. 4): optic nerve atrophy, retinal bleeding and glucoma; with Yangbai (G.B. 14), Chengqi (St. 1) and Hegu (L.I. 4): nebular; with Hegu (L.I. 4), Sibai (St. 2), Fengchi (G.B. 20), Head-Linqi (G.B. 15), Guangming (G.B. 37) and Sizhukong (S.J. 23): pain, swelling and redness of eye; with Ganshu (U.B. 18), Shenshu (U.B. 23), Guangming (G.B. 37) and Taiyang (Extra): night blindness; with Taichong (Liv. 3): central retinitis.

Method: After instructing the patient to look straight ahead, the needle is then inserted straight with a minimum of agitation or twirling, to a depth of 0.5 to 1.5 *cun*. Apply pressure when the needle is withdrawn to avoid bleeding.

Sensation: Local distention and soreness. Tears will flow after the needle is withdrawn.

Zanzhu (U.B. 2)

Location: Above the Jingming (U.B. 1), at the medial end of the eyebrow (See *Fig*. 2-8 on page 34).

Function: Dispersing wind and brightening eye vision.

Indications: Headache, eye diseases, facial paralysis.

Points combination: Zanzhu (U.B. 2) combined with Fengchi (G.B. 20), Taiyang (Extra), Hegu (L.I. 4) and Sizhukong (S.J. 23): acute conjunctivitis and electric ophthalmia; with Ganshu (U.B. 18) and Fengchi (G.B. 20): optic nerve atrophy and retina hemorrhage; with Touwei (St. 8), Yintang (Extra) and Hegu (L.I. 4): frontal headache; with Houxi (S.I. 3) and Yemen (S.J. 2): redness of eyes; with Taiyang (Extra): pain of the first branch of trigeminal nerves, or pain in the supra-orbital region.

Method: Puncture obliquely and inferiorly 0.5-1 *cun* with a local sensation of distension and aching around orbit for the treatment of eye diseases. Puncture horizontally towards Yuyao (Extra) 1-1.5 *cun* with a local sensation of distension and aching at supra-orbital region or the sensation like electric shock radiating to the forehead. Moxibustion is contraindicated.

Shenshu (U.B. 23, Back-Shu Point of the kidney)

Location: Below the 2nd lumbar vertebrae, 1.5 *cun* lateral to the vertebrae, one point on each side.

Function: Benefiting the kidney, strengthening the low back, removing the pathogenic damp and improving hearing.

Indications: Lower back pain, spermatorrhea, impotence, premature ejaculation.

Points combination: Shenshu (U.B. 23) combined with Weizhong (U.B. 40) and Yaoshu (Du 2): low back pain; with Xinshu (U.B. 15), Shenmen (H. 7), Ganshu (U.B. 18) and Fengchi (G.B. 20): headache and insomnia; with Ganshu (U.B. 18), Tinggong (S.I. 19), Yifeng (S.J. 17) and Hand-Zhongzhu (S.J. 3): deafness and ringing in the ears; with Shangliao (U.B. 31), Ciliao (U.B. 32), Zhongliao (U.B. 33) and Xialiao (U.B. 34): irregular menstruation; with Guanyuan (Ren 4), Zhongji (Ren 3) and Sanyinjiao (Sp. 6): spermatorrhea and impotence; with Shuidao (St. 28), Yinlingquan (Sp. 9) and Taixi (K. 3): edema; with Pishu (U.B. 20),

Sanjiaoshu (U.B. 22), Shuiquan (K. 5) and Ququan (Liv. 8): diabetes.

Method: Straight or slanted insertion, needle pointed towards the spine, 1-1.5 *cun*. Moxibustion may be applied for 5-10 minutes.

Dachangshu (U.B. 25, Back-Shu Point of the large intestine)

Location: Below the 5th lumbar vertebrae, 1.5 *cun* lateral to the lower spine.

Function: Relaxing tendons and lower back, removing obstruction in Fu organs.

Indications: Low back pain, abdominal pain.

Points combination: Dachangshu (U.B. 25) combined with Huantiao (G.B. 30), Weizhong (U.B. 40), Yanglingquan (G.B. 34), Sanyinjiao (Sp. 6) and Zusanli (St. 36): sciatica; with Shenshu (U.B. 23), Biguan (St. 31), Xuehai (Sp. 10) and Femur-Futu (St. 32): weakness of thigh and knee; with Xiaochangshu (U.B. 27), Zusanli (St. 36), and Shangjuxu (St. 37): dysentery; with Shenshu (U.B. 23), Weizhong (U.B. 40), Kunlun (U.B. 60) and Xuanzhong (G.B. 39): spondylitis due to osteophytes of lumbar vertebrae; with Xingjian (Liv. 2): acute intestinal obstruction; with Baihuanshu (U.B. 30), puncturing Tiaokou (St. 38) towards Chengshan (U.B. 57), Mingmen (Du 4), puncturing Yanglingquan (G.B. 34) towards Yinlingquan (Sp. 9): progressive muscular malnutrition.

Method: Straight insertion, 1-1.5 *cun*. Moxibustion may be applied for 5-10 minutes.

Weizhong (U.B. 40, He-Sea Point)

Location: At the middle of the transverse crease on the back of the knee.

Function: Relaxing tendons, removing obstruction of vessels, cooling blood, reducing heat, relieving pain of lumbar and knee regions, and stopping vomiting.

Indications: Pain in the lower back, shoulder and leg, paralysis of lower limbs, arthritic pain of the knee joint, heatstroke, acute vomiting and diarrhea, fever.

Points combination: Weizhong (U.B. 40) combined with Shenshu (U.B. 23) and Dachangshu (U.B. 25): low back pain; with Huantiao (G.B. 30), Yanglingquan (G.B. 34) and Sanyinjiao (Sp. 6): paralysis of lower limbs; with bleeding Chize (Lu. 5): acute abdominal pain, vomiting, sunstroke; with Dachangshu (U.B. 25), Huantiao (G.B. 30), Zusanli (St. 36) and Xuanzhong (G.B. 39): sciatica; with Chengshan (U.B. 57), Chengjin (U.B. 56), and Taichong (Liv. 3): spasm of gastrocnimia muscle.

Method: Straight insertion, 1-1.5 *cun*, or may prick to cause a few drops of blood.

Kunlun (U.B. 60, Jing-River Point)

Location: In the depression between the external malleolus and tendo calcaneus.

Function: Expelling wind and removing obstruction from channels, relaxing tendons and strengthening waist, clearing heat from head and eye.

Indications: Pain along the Urinary Bladder Channel, infantile convulsion and epilepsy, difficult labor, constipation.

Points combination: Kunlun (U.B. 60) combined with Fengchi (G.B. 20), Hegu (L.I. 4) and Houxi (S.I. 3): headache; with Qiuxu (G.B. 40), Zhaohai (K. 6) and Taixi (K. 3): heel pain; with Foot-Linqi (G.B. 41), Yinlingquan (Sp. 9) and Shenmen (H. 7): asthma; with Yaoyangguan (Du 3), Mingmen (Du 4), Dachangshu (U.B. 25) and Yinmen (U.B. 37): lumbar spinal pain; with Lingdao (H. 4), Jinggu (U.B. 64), Shendao (Du 11) and Fengfu (Du 16): epilepsy.

Method: Perpendicular insertion 0.5-1 *cun*, with the needle tip pointing towards Taixi (K. 3). Needle sensation is local and radiates down to the sole. Moxibustion is applicable.

Zhiyin (U.B. 67, Jing-Well Point)

Location: On the little toe, 0.1 *cun* from the lower lateral corner of the cuticle of the toenail.

Function: Dispersing wind-heat, clearing heat from head and eye, regulating Qi activities and promoting delivery.

Indications: Difficult labor, malposition of fetus (with moxibustion).

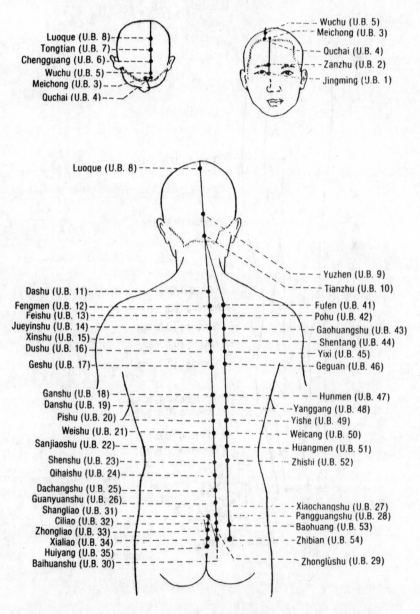

Fig. 2-16a. The Urinary Bladder Channel of Foot-Taiyang.

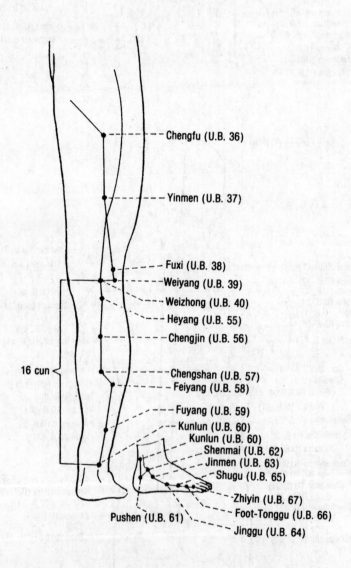

Fig. 2-16b. The Urinary Bladder Channel of Foot-Taiyang.

Points combination: Zhiyin (U.B. 67) combined with Taiyang (Extra) and Lieque (Lu. 7): migraine; with Baihui (Du 20), Dashu (U.B. 11) and Fengchi (G.B. 20): pain and stiffness of neck; with Shenshu (U.B. 23) and Ciliao (U.B. 32): spermatorrhea and dysuria.

Method: Slanted insertion, pointed upward, 0.1 *cun*. Moxibustion with moxa-stick may be applied for 10 minutes until feeling warm.

8. Points of the Kidney Channel of Foot-Shaoyin

Yongquan (K. 1, Jing-Well Point)

Location: In the depression of the mid-sole, between the 2nd and 3rd metatarsal bones (*Fig.* 2-17).

Function: Opening orifices, resuscitation, nourishing Yin and clearing heat, relieving irritability.

Indications: Shock, psychosis, hypertension, heatstroke, headache at the vertex, seizure.

Points combination: Yongquan (K. 1) combined with Renzhong (Du 26): coma of windstroke; with Dazhong (K. 4) and Shuitu (St. 10): sore throat; with Jianli (Ren 11): acute heart pain and anorexia; with Sanyinjiao (Sp. 6): feverish sensation of sole of feet, irritability and insomnia; with Jinggu (U.B. 64) and Chengshan (U.B. 57): muscular spasm of sole of foot; with Guan-

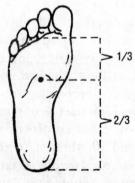

Fig. 2-17.

yuan (Ren 4) and Fenglong (St. 40): cough due to Yin Xu (deficiency).

Method: Straight insertion, 0.5-1 *cun*. Moxibustion may be applied for 3-5 minutes.

Taixi (K. 3, Shu-Stream and Yuan-Source Point)

Location: At the mid-point between the medial malleolus of the ankle and Achilles' tendon.

Function: Nourishing kidney, descending reversed fire, regulating Chong and Ren Channels, clearing heat of the lung and stopping cough.

Indications: Toothache, headache, sore throat, tinnitus, asthma, bleeding caused by cough, irregular, menstruation, spermatorrhea, frequent urination.

Points combination: Taixi (K. 3) combined with Hand-Zhongzhu (S.J. 3) and Shaoze (S.I. 1): sore throat; with Jizhong (Du 6), Mingmen (Du 4) and Yaoyangguan (Du 3): low back pain; with Kunlun (U.B. 60) and Sanyinjiao (Sp. 6): insomnia; with Baihui (Du 20), Taichong (Liv. 3), Shenting (Du 24) and Head-Qiaoyin (G.B. 11): hypertension and dizziness.

Method: Straight insertion, 0.5-1 *cun*. Moxibustion may be applied for 3-5 minutes. Needling sensation may extend towards the foot.

Zhaohai (K. 6, one of the eight confluent points connecting with Yinqiao Channel)

Location: Below the medial malleolus of the ankle.

Function: Relieving sore throat, removing stuffiness of chest, regulating the function of channels and easing the mind.

Indications: Irregular menstruation, sore throat, tinnitus, itching in the genital region, psychosis.

Points combination: Zhaohai (K. 6) combined with Lieque (Lu. 7) forming one pair of eight confluent points: disorders of the lung, throat, chest and diaphragm; with Zhangmen (Liv. 13), Fushe (Sp. 13) and Fuai (Sp. 16): constipation; with Shenmai (U.B. 62): pain and swelling of ankle; with Chize (Lu. 5), Taixi (K. 3) and Xiangu (St. 43): diabetes; with Shenmen (H. 7), Sanyinjiao

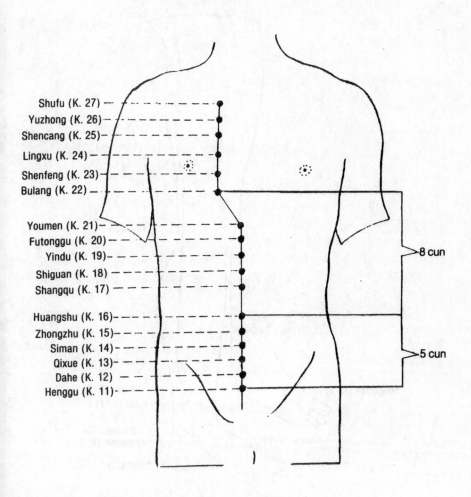

Shufu (K. 27) —
Yuzhong (K. 26) —
Shencang (K. 25) —
Lingxu (K. 24) —
Shenfeng (K. 23) —
Bulang (K. 22) —

Youmen (K. 21) —
Futonggu (K. 20) —
Yindu (K. 19) —
Shiguan (K. 18) —
Shangqu (K. 17) —

Huangshu (K. 16) —
Zhongzhu (K. 15) —
Siman (K. 14) —
Qixue (K. 13) —
Dahe (K. 12) —
Henggu (K. 11) —

8 cun

5 cun

Fig. 2-18a. The Kidney Channel of Foot-Shaoyin

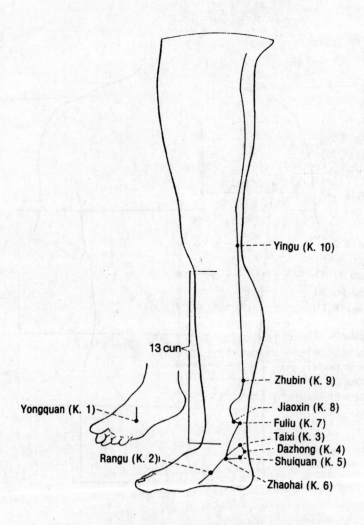

Fig. 2-18b. The Kidney Channel of Foot-Shaoyin.

(Sp. 6), Baihui (Du 20) and Shangxing (Du 23): insomnia; with Guanyuan (Ren 4), Guilai (St. 29) and Baihui (Du 20): uterine prolapse.

Method: Straight insertion, 0.5-1 *cun*. Moxibustion may be applied for 3-5 minutes.

9. Points of the Pericardium Channel of Hand-Jueyin

Ximen (P. 4, Xi-Cleft Point)

Location: Five *cun* directly above the mid-point of the transverse crease of the wrist, between two tendons.

Function: Easing the mind, tranquilizing the heart, clearing eat from Yin system and cooling blood.

Indications: Pain in the chest, arrhythmia, spasm of the diaphragn, psychosis.

Points combination: Ximen (P. 4) combined with Quchi (L.I. 11) and Sanyangluo (S.J. 8): hematemesis; with Shenmen (H. 7) and Sanyinjiao (Sp. 6): insomnia and palpitation; with Yinxi (H. 6), Taichong (Liv. 3) and Neiguan (P. 6): heart pain and irritability.

Method: Straight insertion, 1-1.5 *cun*.

Sensation: Local distension or extending forward.

Neiguan (P. 6, Luo-Connecting Point, one of the eight confluent points communicating with the Yinwei Channel)

Location: Two *cun* above the mid-point of the transverse crease of the wrist, between the two tendons.

Function: Tranquilizing the heart, relieving irritability, regulating Qi circulation, descending rebellious Qi and harmonizing the stomach.

Indications: Pain in the chest and ribs, nauseating, vomiting, hiccups, palpitation, psychosis, stomachache.

Points combination: Neiguan (P. 6) combined with Renzhong (Du 26): coma and aphasia due to windstroke; with Geshu (U.B. 17) and Xinshu (U.B. 15): angina pectoris; with Zhongwan (Ren 12) and Zusanli (St. 36): abdominal pain and vomiting; with Tiantu (Ren 22): hiccough; with Qimen (Liv. 14), Zhangmen (Liv.

13) and Xingjian (Liv. 2): distension, pain and fullness of chest and hypochondriac regions; with Gongsun (Sp. 4) forming one pair of confluent points of the Eight Extra Channels: disorders of the heart, chest and stomach; with Suliao (Du 25): hypotension; with Zusanli (St. 36) and Yongquan (K. 1): toxic shock.

Method: Straight insertion, 0.5-1.5 *cun*, reaching as far as Waiguan (S.J. 5).

Sensation: Local soreness and distension, or distended sensation extending upward and downward.

Laogong (P. 8, Ying-Spring Point)

Location: In the palm between the 3rd and 4th metacarpal bones (*Fig.* 2-19).

Function: Cooling the heart and draining heat.

Indications: Angina pectoris, bleeding of the brain, epistaxis, hand tremors, excessive sweating of the palms, hysterical aphasia.

Points combination: Laogong (P. 8) combined with Renzhong (Du 26) and Hegu (L.I. 4): hysteria; with Yuji (Lu. 10) and Taixi (K. 3): tidal (afternoon) fever; with Fenglong (St. 40), Taichong (Liv. 3), Renzhong (Du 26) and Twelve Jing-Well Points: Tense type of wind-stroke.

Method: Straight insertion, 3-5 *cun*.

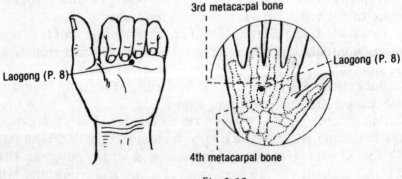

Fig. 2-19.

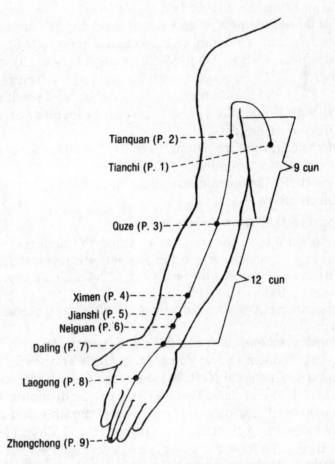

Tianquan (P. 2)

Tianchi (P. 1)

9 cun

Quze (P. 3)

12 cun

Ximen (P. 4)
Jianshi (P. 5)
Neiguan (P. 6)
Daling (P. 7)

Laogong (P. 8)

Zhongchong (P. 9)

Fig. 2-20. The Pericardium Channel of Hand-Jueyin.

10. Points of the Sanjiao Channel of Hand-Shaoyang

Hand-Zhongzhu (S.J. 3, Shu-Stream Point)

Location: With the hand lying prone, this point can be found between the 4th and 5th metacarpal bones, in the hollow behind the metacarpo-phalangeal joint.

Function: Dispersing wind, clearing heat and removing obstruction of the channels.

Indications: Ringing in the ears, deafness, pain in the shoulder

71

and arm, headache, loss of voice.

Points combination: Hand-Zhongzhu (S.J. 3) combined with Ermen (S.J. 21), Tinggong (S.I. 19) and Yifeng (S.J. 17): tinnitus and deafness; with Jiaosun (S.J. 20), Fengchi (G.B. 20) and Head-Qiaoyin (G.B. 11): migraine; with Zhigou (S.J. 6), Neiting (St. 44), Taixi (K. 3) and Shousanli (L.I. 10): soreness and swelling of the throat; with Houxi (S.I. 3) and Hegu (L.I. 4): inability of extension and flexion of fingers.

Method: Straight insertion, 0.3 to 0.8 *cun*. Moxibustion may be applied for 3 to 5 minutes.

Sensation: The needle sensation may possibly extend to fingertips or elbow.

Yangchi (S.J. 4, Yuan-Source Point)

Location: Above the transverse crease on the dorsal surface of the wrist, in a hollow above the 3rd and 4th metacarpal bones.

Function: Harmonizing Shaoyang Channel, clearing heat and subsiding wind.

Indications: Arthritic pain in wrist joint, sore throat, pain in ankle.

Points combination: Yangchi (S.J. 4) combined with Fengmen (U.B. 12), Tianshu (St. 25): headache, chills and fever; with Dazhui (Du 14), Fengchi (G.B. 20) and Hegu (L.I. 4): influenza; with Yangxi (L:I. 5) and Hand-Wangu (S.I. 4): wrist dropping and wrist joint pain; with Zhongwan (Ren 12) and moxibustion on Juque (Ren 14): morning sickness; with Jiquan (H. 1), Chize (Lu. 5) and Taiyuan (Lu. 9): Raynaud's disease.

Method: Puncture perpendicularly 0.3-0.5 *cun* with a local sensation of soreness and distension or puncture obliquely towards both sides 0.5-1 *cun* with a sensation of soreness and distension radiating to the whole joint of the wrist. Moxibustion is applicable.

Waiguan (S.J. 5, Luo-Connecting Point)

Location: Two *cun* above the transverse crease of the dorsal surface of the wrist, between the ulna and radius.

Function: Dispersing wind and removing obstruction from the channels; also an important point for stopping pain of the upper limb.

Indications: Pain in forearm, numbness, headache, tinnitus, cold, fever, stiff neck, parotitis.

Points combination: Waiguan (S.J. 5) combined with Tinggong (S.I. 19) and Taixi (K. 3): deafness and tinnitus; with Neiguan (P. 6) and Yangfu (G.B. 38): hypochondriac pain: with Foot-Linqi (G.B. 41) and Hegu (L.I. 4): fever of common cold; with Jianyu (L.I. 15), Quchi (L.I. 11) and Quze (P. 3): paralysis of the upper limbs; with Foot-Linqi (G.B. 41) alone forming one of the pairs of the Eight Confluent Points: disorders of outer canthus, retroauricle, cheek, neck and shoulder regions; with Yanglao (S.I. 6): severe shoulder pain.

Method: Puncture perpendicularly 1-1.5 *cun* towards Neiguan (P. 6) with a local sensation of soreness and distension first, sometimes radiating to the tips of the 3rd, 4th and 5th fingers, or puncture obliquely and upward 1-2 *cun* with a local sensation of soreness and distension first, then radiating to the elbow and shoulder regions. Moxibustion is applicable.

Zhigou (S.J. 6, Jing-River Point)

Location: 3 *cun* above the dorsal transverse crease of the wrist, between the ulna radius.

Function: Clearing the heat from Sanjiao, removing obstruction of the channel, regulating the Qi circulation of Fu organs and relieving discomfort of hypochondriac region.

Indications: Hypochondriac pain, constipation, fever without sweating, ringing in the ears, deafness, sudden hoarseness of voice.

Points combination: Zhigou (S.J. 6) combined with Yanglingquan (G.B. 34): intercostal neuralgia; with Yanglingquan (G.B. 34) and Riyue (G.B. 24): cholecystitis; with Zusanli (St. 36), Tianshu (St. 25) and Daheng (Sp. 15): habitual constipation; with Quchi (L.I. 11), Dazhui (Du 14) and Zhongchong (P. 9): fever without perspiration.

Method: Puncture perpendicularly 1-1.5 *cun* with a local sensation of soreness and distension or the sensation radiating to the wrist and elbow regions. Moxibustion is applicable.

Jianliao (S.J. 14)

Location: one *cun* in the depression just posterior and inferior to the acromion of the shoulder (See *Fig.* 2-5 on page 29).

Function: Expelling wind and damp, and removing obstruction from channels.

Indications: Difficulty in raising shoulder, pain and heaviness in shoulder.

Points combination: Jianliao (S.J. 14) combined with Quchi (L.I. 11), Tianzong (S.I. 11) and Yanggu (S.I. 5): inability of raising the arm; with Jianyu (L.I. 15) and Yanglao (S.I. 6): arm pain; with Jianzhen (S.I. 9) and Jianyu (L.I. 15): shoulder joint pain.

Method: Perpendicular insertion with needle pointing towards the shoulder joint 1-1.5 *cun*.

Yifeng (S.J. 17)

Location: In the depression behind the earlobe.

Function: Removing wind and reducing heat, improving hearing, promoting the circulation of blood and Qi in the channels.

Indications: Deafness, ringing in the ears, deaf-mutism, parotitis, sore eyes.

Points combination: Yifeng (S.J. 17) combined with Tinggong (S.I. 19) and Hand-Zhongzhu (S.J. 3): deafness and tinnitus; with Dicang (St. 4), Jiache (St. 6), Sibai (St. 2) and Hegu (L.I. 4): facial paralysis; with Xiaguan (St. 7) and Hegu (L.I. 4): clenched teeth.

Method: Slanted insertion 0.5 to 1.5 *cun* needle pointed inward from back to front, distension at the bottom of the ear and ear canal, when inserted 1 *cun*. Sometimes soreness extends to the bottom of the ear, and hotness in part of the face.

Jiaosun (S.J. 20)

Location: Directly above the ear apex.

Function: Clearing heat and dispersing wind.

Indications: Ear diseases.

Points combination: Jiaosun (S.J. 20) combined with Jiache (St. 6), Xiaguan (St. 7) and Sanjian (L.I. 3): toothache; with Neiting (St. 44), Chongyang (St. 42) and Hegu (L.I. 4): pain and swelling of gums; with Ganshu (U.B. 18), Fengchi (G.B. 20) and Taiyang

(Extra): optic neuritis; with Shaoshang (Lu. 11) and Quchi (L.I. 11): pimples and eczema.

Method: Vertical insertion, 3 to 5 *cun*.

Ermen (S.J. 21)

Location: At the front of the tuberculum supra-tragicum, in the depression formed when the mouth is open.

Function: Clearing heat and opening orifices.

Indications: Tinnitus, deafness, toothache.

Points combination: Ermen (S.J. 21) combined with Hand-Zhongzhu (S.J. 3) and Waiguan (S.J. 5): tinnitus and diplacusis; with Sizhukong (S.J. 23), Jiache (St. 6) and Zusanli (St. 36): toothache and ear pain.

Method: Puncture perpendicularly 0.5-2 *cun* or obliquely downward 1.5-2 *cun* with the mouth open. A local sensation of soreness and distension radiating to the opposite side can be obtained. Moxibustion is advisable.

Sizhukong (S.J. 23)

Location: At the lateral end of the eyebrow (See *Fig.* 2-8 on page 34).

Function: Clearing heat from head and facial regions, dispersing wind and brightening vision.

Indications: Headache, eye diseases, facial paralysis, spasm of the eye muscle.

Points combination: Sizhukong (S.J. 23) combined with Renzhong (Du 26) and Baihui (Du 20): epilepsy; with Zanzhu (U.B. 2), Taiyang (Extra) and Sibai (St. 2): redness, swelling and pain of eyes; with Fengchi (G.B. 20) and Chengqi (St. 1): twitching of eyelids; with Hand-Zhongzhu (S.J. 3) and Fengchi (G.B. 20): migraine; with Dicang (St. 4) and Sibai (St. 2): facial paralysis.

Method: Transverse insertion, 0.8 to 1.5 *cun*, either towards the canthus or outward.

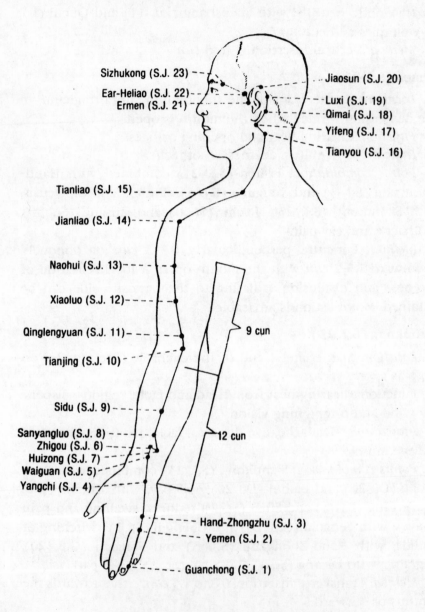

Sizhukong (S.J. 23)

Ear-Heliao (S.J. 22)
Ermen (S.J. 21)

Jiaosun (S.J. 20)

Luxi (S.J. 19)
Qimai (S.J. 18)
Yifeng (S.J. 17)
Tianyou (S.J. 16)

Tianliao (S.J. 15)

Jianliao (S.J. 14)

Naohui (S.J. 13)

Xiaoluo (S.J. 12)

Qinglengyuan (S.J. 11)

Tianjing (S.J. 10)

9 cun

Sidu (S.J. 9)

Sanyangluo (S.J. 8)
Zhigou (S.J. 6)
Huizong (S.J. 7)
Waiguan (S.J. 5)
Yangchi (S.J. 4)

12 cun

Hand-Zhongzhu (S.J. 3)
Yemen (S.J. 2)

Guanchong (S.J. 1)

Fig. 2-21. The Sanjiao Channel of Hand-Shaoyang.

76

11. Points of the Gall Bladder Channel of Foot-Shaoyang

Tinghui (G.B. 2)

Location: 0.5 *cun* below Tinggong (S.I. 19).

Function: Removing obstruction of channels, activating blood circulation, opening orifices and promoting hearing, clearing heat from the liver and gall bladder.

Indications: Similar to those of Tinggong (S.I. 19).

Points combination: Tinghui (G.B. 2) combined with Zhangmen (Liv. 13), Yifeng (S.J. 17) and Waiguan (S.J. 5): deafness and tinnitus; with Yifeng (S.J. 17), Jiache (St. 6), Dicang (St. 4) and Xiaguan (St. 7): deviated mouth and eye; with Xiaguan (St. 7): lower mandibular arthritis; with Tinggong (S.I. 19) and Hand-Zhongzhu (S.J. 3): deafness.

Method: Straight insertion 1 to 1.5 *cun* with mouth open.

Shuaigu (G.B. 8)

Location: Superior to the apex of the auricle, 1.5 *cun* within the hairline.

Function: Dispersing wind, clearing heat and harmonizing the middle Jiao.

Indications: One-sided headache, eye diseases.

Points combination: Shuaigu (G.B. 8) combined with Sizhukong (S.J. 23) and Foot-Linqi (G.B. 41): migraine; with Fengchi (G.B. 20), Taiyang (Extra) and Hand-Zhongzhu (S.J. 3): heaviness of head and dizziness; with Taichong (Liv. 3): acute infantile convulsion.

Method: Puncture horizontally and anteriorly or posteriorly for 0.3-0.5 *cun* with a local sensation of soreness and distension. Moxibustion is applicable.

Yangbai (G.B. 14)

Location: One *cun* above the middle of the eyebrow on a line directly above the pupil of the eye, in the depression on the superciliary arch.

Function: Dispersing wind, clearing heat and brightening vision.

Indications: Facial paralysis, twitching of the eyelids, sore eyes, trigeminal and supra-orbital neuralgia.

Points combination: Yangbai (G.B. 14) combined with Ganshu (U.B. 18), Shenshu (U.B. 23), Fengchi (G.B. 20) and Jingming (U.B. 1): night blindness; with Zanzhu (U.B. 2), Taiyang (Extra) and Shangxing (Du 23): frontal headache; with Yifeng (S.J. 17), Sibai (St. 2), Dicang (St. 4) and Jiache (St. 6): facial paralysis; with Yuyao (Extra) and Zanzhu (U.B. 2): drooping eyelids; with Foot-Qiaoyin (G.B. 44), Yuzhen (U.B. 9) and Naohu (Du 17): pain of the eyeball; with Zanzhu (U.B. 2), Hegu (L.I. 4) and Fuliu (K. 7): allergy in eye.

Method: Puncture horizontally 0.5-1 *cun* with a local sensation of soreness and distension. Moxibustion is allowed.

Fengchi (G.B. 20)

Location: Between the hollow below the tuberosity of the occipital bone at the back of the head and the mastoid process, and parallel to the earlobe.

Function: Resuscitation and opening of orifices blocked by pathogenic factors, expelling wind and relieving exterior symptoms, clearing heat from head and eye, activating blood circulation and removing obstruction from channels.

Indications: Vertigo, headache, eye diseases, ringing in the ears, common cold.

Points combination: Fengchi (G.B. 20) combined with Baihui (Du 20) and Taichong (Liv. 3): vertex headache, dizziness and vertigo; with Hegu (L.I. 4), Taiyang (Extra) and Touwei (St. 8): migraine; with Dazhui (Du 14) and Quchi (L.I. 11): chills and fever of common cold; with Houxi (S.I. 3): pain and stiffness of neck; with Lianquan (Ren 23): aphasia of wind-stroke, dysphagia and dysphonia caused by bulbar palsy; with Renzhong (Du 26), Baihui (Du 20), Shangxing (Du 23), Neiguan (P. 6) and Sanyinjiao (Sp. 6): disorders of cerebrovascular system; with Ganshu (U.B. 18), Shenshu (U.B. 23), Taiyang (Extra) and Guangming (G.B. 37): optic nerve atrophy.

Method: Slanted insertion 0.5 to 1 *cun*, the needle pointed towards the tip of nose. Transverse insertion 2 to 3 *cun* through opposite Fengchi (G.B. 20) (for cerebral arteriosclerosis). Sensation sometimes extends the eye, with slanted insertion towards the nose.

Huantiao (G.B. 30)

Location: On lateral side of the thigh, in the hollow of the greater trochanter. Let the patient lie on his side with legs bent a little. At a point situated one-third of the distance on a line drawn from the greater trochanter of the femur to the sacral hiatus.

Function: Dispersing wind and damp, removing obstruction from channels.

Indications: Sciatica, hemiplegia, numbness in lower limb, infantile paralysis.

Points combination: Huantiao (G.B. 30) combined with Dachangshu (U.B. 25), Zhibian (U.B. 54), Weizhong (U.B. 40) and Yanglingquan (G.B. 34): sciatica; with Weizhong (U.B. 40), Sanyinjiao (Sp. 6) and Yanglingquan (G.B. 34): paralysis of the lower limbs; with Shenshu (U.B. 23) and Weizhong (U.B. 40): low back pain; with Femur-Juliao (G.B. 29) and Zhiyin (U.B. 67): arthritis of hip region; with Yanglingquan (G.B. 34) and Jugu (L.I. 16): pain of the lateral side of lower leg.

Method: Straight insertion, 1-4 *cun*. Local needling sensation extends towards tip of the toe or the sole.

Fengshi (G.B. 31)

Location: Below the tip of the middle finger when in standing position, with the arm extended at the side of the leg.

Function: Dispelling wind, removing the obstruction from the channels and strengthening the tendons and bones.

Indications: Hemiplegia, sciatica, arthritic pain in knee joint.

Points combination: Fengshi (G.B. 31) combined with Huantiao (G.B. 30), Zusanli (St. 36), Sanyinjiao (Sp. 6) and Shenshu (U.B. 23): paralysis of lower limbs; with Quchi (L.I. 11) and Yanglingquan (G.B. 34): cholera; with Yinlingquan (Sp. 9) and Gongsun (Sp. 4): beriberi.

Method: Puncture perpendicularly 1.5-2.5 *cun* with a local sensation of soreness and distension which may radiate downward. Moxibustion is applicable.

79

Yanglingquan (G.B. 34, He-Sea Point, Influential Point of tendons)

Location: At lateral side of the leg in the hollow anterior and below the head of the fibula (*Fig. 2-22*).

Function: Promoting free flow of Qi in the liver and gall bladder, reducing heat and removing damp, relaxing tendons and activating blood circulation of channels.

Indications: Pain in lower back and leg, hemiplegia, coldness and pain in lower limbs, numbness, spasm, stiff neck, hypertension, habitual constipation.

Points combination: Yanglingquan (G.B. 34) combined with Dachangshu (U.B. 25), Huantiao (G.B. 30) and Weizhong (U.B. 40): sciatica; with Fuxi (U.B. 38), Zusanli (St. 36), Jiexi (St. 41) and Xuanzhong (G.B. 39): injury of nervous peroneus communis;

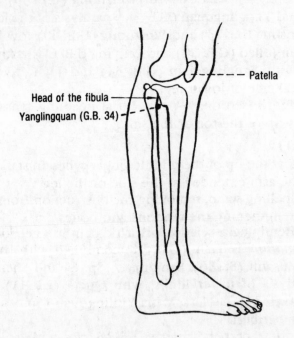

Fig. 2-22.

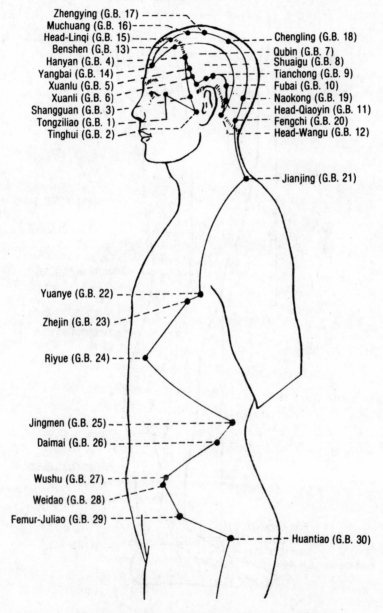

Zhengying (G.B. 17)
Muchuang (G.B. 16)
Head-Linqi (G.B. 15)
Benshen (G.B. 13)
Hanyan (G.B. 4)
Yangbai (G.B. 14)
Xuanlu (G.B. 5)
Xuanli (G.B. 6)
Shangguan (G.B. 3)
Tongziliao (G.B. 1)
Tinghui (G.B. 2)

Chengling (G.B. 18)
Qubin (G.B. 7)
Shuaigu (G.B. 8)
Tianchong (G.B. 9)
Fubai (G.B. 10)
Naokong (G.B. 19)
Head-Qiaoyin (G.B. 11)
Fengchi (G.B. 20)
Head-Wangu (G.B. 12)

Jianjing (G.B. 21)

Yuanye (G.B. 22)

Zhejin (G.B. 23)

Riyue (G.B. 24)

Jingmen (G.B. 25)

Daimai (G.B. 26)

Wushu (G.B. 27)

Weidao (G.B. 28)

Femur-Juliao (G.B. 29)

Huantiao (G.B. 30)

Fig. 2-23a. The Gall Bladder Channel of Foot-Shaoyang.

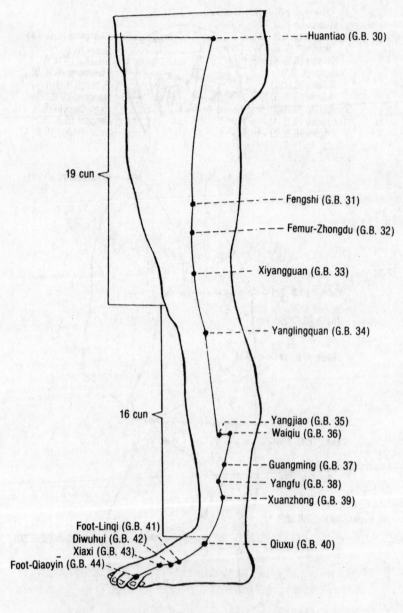

Fig. 2-23b. The Gall Bladder Channel of Foot-Shaoyang.

with Zusanli (St. 36), Huantiao (G.B. 30), Femur-Futu (St. 32) and Sanyinjiao (Sp. 6): hemiplegia and paralysis; with Feishu (U.B. 13), Ganshu (U.B. 18), Danshu (U.B. 19), Riyue (G.B. 24) and Neiguan (P. 6): cholecystitis; with Zhigou (S.J. 6), Zhangmen (Liv. 13) and Foot-Linqi (G.B. 41): hypochondriac pain; with Quchi (L.I. 11), Hegu (L.I. 4) and Taichong (Liv. 3): infantile convulsion; with Zusanli (St. 36) and Gongsun (Sp. 4): abdominal distension; with Yinlingquan (Sp. 9): Malaria.

Method: Straight insertion, 1-3 *cun*, may join Yanglingquan (G.B. 34).

Sensation: Needling sensation may extend to foot, sometimes to shoulder.

Xuanzhong (G.B. 39, Influential Point of Marrow)

Location: Three *cun* above the lateral malleolus of the ankle, anterior to the fibula.

Function: Dispelling wind and damp, relaxing tendons and bones.

Indications: Stiff neck, paralysis, beriberi, pain of the lower limb, weakness of the lower limbs, arthritic pain in ankle joint.

Points combination: Xuanzhong (G.B. 39) combined with Huantiao (G.B. 30), Yanglingquan (G.B. 34), Weizhong (U.B. 40) and Sanyinjiao (Sp. 6): hemiplegia; with Tianzhu (U.B. 10), Houxi (S.I. 3) and Fengchi (G.B. 20): stiffness of neck; with Fengchi (G.B. 20) and Foot-Linqi (G.B. 41): headache; with Yanglingquan (G.B. 34), Zusanli (St. 36), Jiexi (St. 41) and Taichong (Liv. 3): Wei and Bi syndromes of lower limbs.

Method: Straight insertion, 0.5-1.5 *cun*. Needling sensation may extend downward to the foot and up to the shoulder and neck.

12. Points of the Liver Channel of Foot-Jueyin

Taichong (Liv. 3, Shu-Stream and Yuan-Source Point)

Location: On the foot, 2 *cun* above the web between the 1st and 2nd toes.

Function: Reducing fire of the liver, brightening vision, clearing heat of the heart, easing the mind, regulating Qi circulation and harmonizing blood circulation.

Indications: Headache, dizziness, vertigo, toothache, sore and congested throat, hysteria, convulsions, amenorrhea and dysmenorrhea.

Points combination: Taichong (Liv. 3) combined with Fengchi (G.B. 20), Zusanli (St. 36) and Sanyinjiao (Sp. 6): dizziness and vertigo; with Baihui (Du 20): vertex headache; with Sanyinjiao (Sp. 6), Xuehai (Sp. 10) and Guanyuan (Ren 4): uterine bleeding; with Quchi (L.I. 11), Neiguan (P. 6) and Zusanli (St. 36): hypertension; with Baihui (Du 20), Renzhong (Du 26) and Hegu (L.I. 4): mania, depression, and epilepsy; with Hegu (L.I. 4): insomnia due to Yin deficiency.

Method: Straight insertion, 0.5-1 *cun*.

Sensation: Distension and soreness in the two toes, or extending towards the abdomen.

Ququan (Liv. 8, He-Sea Point)

Location: Knee flexed, the point is in the depression above the medial end of the transverse popliteal crease, posterior to the medial condyle of the tibia, between m. semimembranosus and m. semitendinosus.

Function: Activating channel and eliminating damp heat.

Indications: Dysuria, seminal emission, vulvitis, irregular menstruation, leukorrhea, prolapse of uterus.

Points combination: Ququan (Liv. 8) combined with Baihui (Du 20), Qihai (Ren 6) and Sanyinjiao (Sp. 6): prolapse of uterus; with Xuehai (Sp. 10) and Ligou (Liv. 5): pruritus in vulva; with Guilai (St. 29), Zhongji (Ren 3) and Taichong (Liv. 3): pain in penis, hernias; with Xingjian (Liv. 2): retention of urine.

Method: Puncture perpendicularly 1-1.5 *cun* with distension sensation locally. Moxibustion is applicable.

Jimai (Liv. 12)

Location: 2.5 *cun* lateral to Ren Channel, at groin.

Function: Regulating the function of the liver and eliminating cold and damp.

Indications: Hernia, prolapse of uterus, pain in the vulva, lower abdomen and medial side of thigh.

Points combination: Jimai (Liv. 12) combined with Zusanli (St. 36), Sanyinjiao (Sp. 6): pain in the lower abdomen; with Xuehai (Sp. 10), Yinlingquan (Sp. 9): pain in the medial side of thigh; with Dadun (Liv. 1) and Guanyuan (Ren 4): orehitis, edema in the testes, pain in the penis or vagina.

Method: Puncture perpendicularly 0.5-0.8 *cun*. Avoid femoral artery.

Sensation: Local distension and soreness, or extending towards the vulva. Moxibustion is not applicable.

Zhangmen (Liv. 13, Front-Mu Point of the spleen, it is one of the Eight Confluent Points dominating the Zang organs)

Location: Below the tree end of the 11th floating rib.

Function: Promoting the function of the liver, strengthening the spleen, stopping vomiting and diarrhea.

Indications: Hypochondriac pain, jaundice, vomiting, diarrhea.

Points combination: Zhangmen (Liv. 13) combined with Zhongwan (Ren 12), Zusanli (St. 36), Qihai (Ren 6): abdominal distension; with Shidou (Sp. 17), Zhigou (S.J. 6), Yanglingquan (G.B. 34): hypochondriac pain; with Tianshu (St. 25), Shangjuxu (St. 37): borborygmus, diarrhea; with Neiguan (P. 6), Zhongwan (Ren 12), Neiting (St. 44): vomiting, indigestion; with Shuidao (St. 28), Shuifen (Ren 9), Yinlingquan (Sp. 9): ascites; with Weizhong (U.B. 40), Shenshu (U.B. 23): lumbago.

Method: Puncture perpendicularly 0.5-0.8 *cun* with distension and soreness locally. Moxibustion is applicable.

Qimen (Liv. 14, Front-Mu Point of liver)

Location: On the mammillary line, four *cun* lateral to Ren Channel. In the 6th intercostal space.

Function: Regulating functions of the liver and spleen, promoting circulation of Qi and blood.

Indications: Pain in the chest and hypochondriac area, abdominal distension, fullness of the chest, vomiting, hiccup, pain in the nipple.

Points combination: Qimen (Liv. 14) combined with Shan-

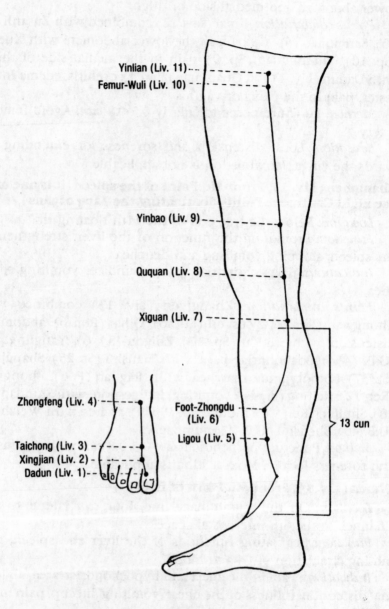

Yinlian (Liv. 11)

Femur-Wuli (Liv. 10)

Yinbao (Liv. 9)

Ququan (Liv. 8)

Xiguan (Liv. 7)

Zhongfeng (Liv. 4)

Foot-Zhongdu
(Liv. 6)

Ligou (Liv. 5)

13 cun

Taichong (Liv. 3)

Xingjian (Liv. 2)

Dadun (Liv. 1)

Fig. 2-24a. The Liver Channel of Foot-Jueyin.

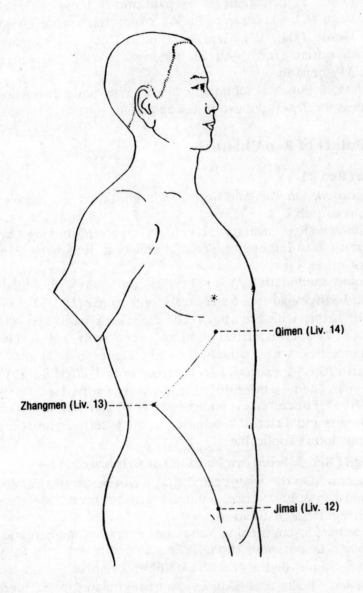

Qimen (Liv. 14)

Zhangmen (Liv. 13)

Jimai (Liv. 12)

Fig. 2-24b. The Liver Channel of Foot-Jueyin.

zhong (Ren 17), Neiguan (P. 6): pain and fullness in the chest; with Hegu (L.I. 4), Zusanli (St. 36): stomachache, borborygmus; with Geshu (U.B. 17), Ganshu (U.B. 18), Zhongfeng (Liv. 4): hypochondriac pain; with Zhongfeng (Liv. 4), Yanglingquan (G.B. 34): hepatitis.

Method: Puncture obliquely 0.3-0.5 *cun* with distension or soreness locally. Moxibustion is applicable.

13. Points of Ren Channel

Qugu (Ren 2)

Location: On the mid-line of the abdomen just above the symphysis pubis.

Function: Replenishing the kidney and strengthening Yang.

Indications: Impotence, seminal emission, leukorrhea, retention of urine.

Points combination: Qugu (Ren 2) combined with Guilai (St. 29) and Sanyinjiao (Sp. 6): enuresis; with Jimai (Liv. 12): retention of urine; with Shenshu (U.B. 23), Guanyuan (Ren 4) and Fuliu (K. 7): spermatorrhea and impotence; with Dadun (Liv. 1): dysmenorrhea; with Daimai (G.B. 26), Ligou (Liv. 5) and Yinlingquan (Sp. 9): excessive leukorrhea; with Guilai (St. 29) and Guanyuan (Ren 4): infertility due to oviduct adhesion.

Method: Puncture perpendicularly 2-2.5 *cun* with a sensation of soreness and distension radiating to the external genital organ. Moxibustion is applicable.

Zhongji (Ren 3, Front-Mu Point of the urinary bladder)

Location: On the anterior mid-line, 4 *cun* below the umbilicus.

Indications: Impotence, seminal emission, premature ejaculation, irregular menstruation.

Function: Strengthening Yang and regulating menstruation.

Points combination: Zhongji (Ren 3) combined with Sanyinjiao (Sp. 6) and Baihui (Du 20): children's enuresis; with Guanyuan (Ren 4), Shenshu (U.B. 23) and Sanyinjiao (Sp. 6): spermatorrhea; with Ciliao (U.B. 32), Xuehai (Sp. 10) and Sanyinjiao (Sp. 6): irregular menstruation and uterine bleeding; with Zhibian

(U.B. 54), Changqiang (Du 1) and Taixi (K. 3): prostatitis.

Method: Straight insertion, 1-2 *cun*. Needling sensation may extend to genitals and perineum. Moxibustion may be applied for 5-10 minutes.

Guanyuan (Ren 4, Front-Mu Point of the small intestine)

Location: Three *cun* below the navel.

Function: Warming the kidney, strengthening Yang and regulating Chong and Ren channels.

Indications: Impotence, premature ejaculation, seminal emission, enuresis, frequency of micturition, pain with urination, retention of urine, irregular menstruation, leukorrhea, diarrhea, dysentery.

Points combination: Guanyuan (Ren 4) combined with Shenshu (U.B. 23), Renzhong (Du 26), Neiguan (P. 6), Zhongwan (Ren 12) and Sanyinjiao (Sp. 6): spermatorrhea, impotence and enuresis; with Tianshu (St. 25), Zusanli (St. 36), Xiaochangshu (U.B. 27) and Dachangshu (U.B. 25): abdominal pain and diarrhea; with Jimai (Liv. 12), Zhongji (Ren 3) and Zhangmen (Liv. 13): bleeding of the urinary bladder; with Zusanli (St. 36) plus moxibustion: tonification of the whole body.

Method: Straight insertion, 1-1.5 *cun*. Needling sensation may extend to penis.

Qihai (Ren 6)

Location: 1.5 *cun* below the navel.

Function: Warming and reinforcing the lower Jiao.

Indications: Abdominal pain, diarrhea, prolapse of the anus, enuresis, irregular menstruation, prolapsed uterus.

Points combination: Qihai (Ren 6) combined with Sanyinjiao (Sp. 6) and Dadun (Liv. 1): dysmenorrhea; with Shenshu (U.B. 23) and Zusanli (St. 36): weak body emaciation; with Shanzhong (Ren 17), Shenshu (U.B. 23), Feishu (U.B. 13) and Taiyuan (Lu. 9): shortness of breath and dyspnea; with Tianshu (St. 25), Zhongwan (Ren 12) and Shangjuxu (St. 37): fullness and distension of the abdomen; with Guanyuan (Ren 4), Sanyinjiao (Sp. 6) and Weidao (G.B. 28): uterine prolapse.

Method: Straight insertion, 1-1.5 *cun*. Needling sensation extends downward.

Shenque (Ren 8)

Location: In the center of the navel.

Function: Warming Yang, relieving collapse, regulating the spleen and harmonizing the stomach.

Indications: Borborygmus, diarrhea, dysentery, flaccid type of apoplexy, prolapse of the anus.

Points combination: Shenque (Ren 8) combined with Zusanli (St. 36), Tianshu (St. 25) and Guanyuan (Ren 4): borborygmus and diarrhea; with Changqiang (Du 1), Qihai (Ren 6) and Baihui (Du 20): anus prolapse;

Method: Puncture is contraindicated. Moxibustion is applied for 5-15 minutes.

Zhongwan (Ren 12, Front-Mu Point of the stomach, Influential Point of Fu organ)

Location: Four *cun* above the navel.

Function: Building up the spleen, removing damp, regulating Qi circulation, stopping pain, descending reversed Qi and harmonizing the stomach.

Indications: Stomachache, abdominal distension, vomiting, borborygmus, diarrhea, dysentery.

Points combination: Zhongwan (Ren 12) combined with Liangmen (St. 21), Tianshu (St. 25), Shuidao (St. 28), Qihai (Ren 6), Baihui (Du 20) and Zusanli (St. 36): gastroptosis; with Sifeng (Extra) and Yanglingquan (G.B. 34): biliary ascariasis; with Quchi (L.I. 11), Shangjuxu (St. 37) and Tianshu (St. 25): dysentery and acute appendicitis; with Liangqiu (St. 34) and Neiguan (P. 6): gastric pain; with Gongsun (Sp. 4), Neiguan (P. 6), Tianshu (St. 25) and Zusanli (St. 36): disorders of intestines and stomach; with Riyue (G.B. 24), Yanglingquan (G.B. 34): cholecystitis.

Method: Straight insertion 0.8-2.5 *cun*.

Sensation: Local distension and numbness. Moxibustion may be applied for 5-10 minutes.

Shanzhong (Ren 17, Front-Mu Point of the pericardium, Influential Point of Qi)

Location: In the middle level with the nipples of the breasts, in the hollow of the 4th rib.

Function: Broadening chest, regulating Qi circulation, descending reversed Qi and dissolving phlegm.

Indications: Asthma, difficulty or inability to swallow, pain in the chest, insufficient lactation, hiccups.

Points combination: Shanzhong (Ren 17) combined with Xinshu (U.B. 15), Jueyinshu (U.B. 14), Yinxi (H. 6) and Neiguan (P. 6): angina pectoris; with Tiantu (Ren 22), Feishu (U.B. 13), Chize (Lu. 5) and Lieque (Lu. 7): cough and asthma; with Shaoze (S.I. 1) and Yemen (S.J. 2): insufficient lactation; with Tiantu (Ren 22): mastitis; with Geshu (U.B. 17) and Neiguan (P. 6): fullness of chest and hypochondriac regions, hiccough.

Method: Straight insertion, 0.3-0.5 *cun*. Transverse insertion upward or downward, 0.5-1.5 *cun*.

Tiantu (Ren 22)

Location: In the middle of the depression above the suprasternal notch.

Function: Descending reversed Qi, dissolving phlegm, clearing heat from the throat.

Indications: Asthma, cough, sore throat, throat diseases.

Points combination: Tiantu (Ren 22) combined with Feishu (U.B. 13) and Kongzui (Lu. 6): cough and asthma; with Neiguan (P. 6): hiccup; with Lianquan (Ren 23) and Tongli (H. 5): aphasia; with Yintang (Extra), Zusanli (St. 36) and Neiguan (P. 6): neural vomiting; with Lieque (Lu. 7) and Zhaohai (K. 6): globus hystericus.

Method: First insert perpendicularly, then needle downward along the posterior side of the manubrium sterni, anterior to the trachea, approximately 1-1.5 *cun*, local distension and a constricted sensation around the pharynx.

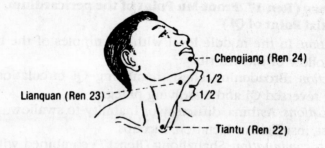

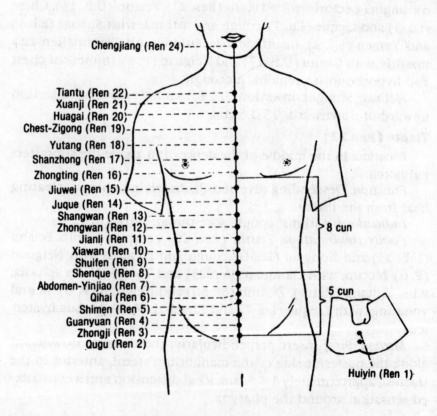

Fig. 2-25. The Ren Channel.

14. Points of Du Channel

Yaoyangguan (Du 3)

Location: Below the spinous process of the 4th lumbar vertebrae.

Function: Warming the lower Jiao, strengthening lumbar spine and dispelling cold-damp.

Indications: Pain in the lumbosacral region, muscular atrophy, motor impairment, numbness and pain of the lower limbs, irregular menstruation, seminal emission, impotence and hemorrhoids.

Points combination: Yaoyangguan (Du 3) combined with Shenshu (U.B. 23), Weizhong (U.B. 40) and Kunlun (U.B. 60): lumbar spinal pain; with Huantiao (G.B. 30), Dachangshu (U.B. 25) and Yanglingquan (G.B. 34): paralysis and pain of the lower limbs; with Ciliao (U.B. 32), Guanyuan (Ren 4) and Sanyinjiao (Sp. 6): impotence, seminal emission, irregular menstruation and leukorrhea.

Method: Perpendicular insertion 0.8-1 *cun*. Needle sensation is local distension.

Mingmen (Du 4)

Location: Below the 14th vertebrae (or below the 2nd lumbar vertebrae).

Function: Nourishing the Primary (Yuan) Qi and strengthening the kidney, benefiting the lumbar vertebrae.

Indications: Low back pain, enuresis, leukorrhea, impotence.

Points combination: Mingmen (Du 4) combined with Dazhui (Du 14), Ganshu (U.B. 18), Quchi (L.I. 11) and Zusanli (St. 36): iron deficiency anemia; with Baihui (Du 20), Guanyuan (Ren 4), Sanyinjiao (Sp. 6) and Zhongliao (U.B. 33): enuresis (use moxibustion); with Shenshu (U.B. 23): copious urine in the elderly.

Method: Perpendicular insertion for 0.5-1 *cun*. Moxibustion may be applied for 5-10 minutes.

Dazhui (Du 14)

Location: Above the 1st thoracic vertebrae.

Function: Relieving exterior syndromes and opening the Yang, clearing the brain and calming the mind.

Indications: Acute fever, malaria, seizure, bronchitis, asthma, pain in neck, stiff back.

Points combination: Dazhui (Du 14) combined with Fengchi (G.B. 20) and Quchi (L.I. 11): influenza; with Feishu (U.B. 13) and Fenglong (St. 40): bronchitis; with Hegu (L.I. 4), Quchi (L.I. 11), Zusanli (St. 36), Pishu (U.B. 20) and Sanyinjiao (Sp. 6): leukopenia; with Feishu (U.B. 13) and Zusanli (St. 36): eosinophilia; with Yaoshu (Du 2): tidal fever.

Method: Perpendicular insertion 0.5-1 *cun*. Needling sensation extends downward, or up towards the head and either side of shoulders.

Baihui (Du 20)

Location: At the intersection of the median line at the vertex of head with a line drawn from the tip of one ear to the other (*Fig.* 2-26).

Function: Resuscitation, removing wind, restoring collapsed Yang, clearing heat and easing the mind.

Indications: Headache, dizziness, shock, prolapsed anus, prolapsed uterus, insomnia.

Points combination: Baihui (Du 20) combined with Fengchi (G.B. 20), Hegu (L.I. 4), Quchi (L.I. 11) and Dazhui (Du 14): high fever and headache; with Renzhong (Du 26) and Neiguan (P. 6): coma; with Chengshan (U.B. 57) and Changqiang (Du 1): anus prolapse; with Guanyuan (Ren 4), Ciliao (U.B. 32), Qihai (Ren 6) and Shenshu (U.B. 23): uterine prolapse; with Zhongwan (Ren 12), Qihai (Ren 6), Tianshu (St. 25) and Zusanli (St. 36): gastroptosis; with Taichong (Liv. 3), Houxi (S.I. 3) and Tianshu (St. 25): dizziness and vertigo; with Shenmen (H. 7), Yifeng (S.J. 17) and Shangxing (Du 23): insomnia; moxibustion on Baihui (Du 20): Meniere's syndrome.

Method: Transverse insertion, front to back, 0.3 to 0.5 *cun*. Moxibustion for 5 to 10 minutes.

Renzhong (Du 26, also known as Shuigou)

Location: In the philtrum, approximately one-third the distance from the bottom of the nose to the top of the lip (*Fig.* 2-26).

Function: Dispersing wind, opening orifices and stopping pain.

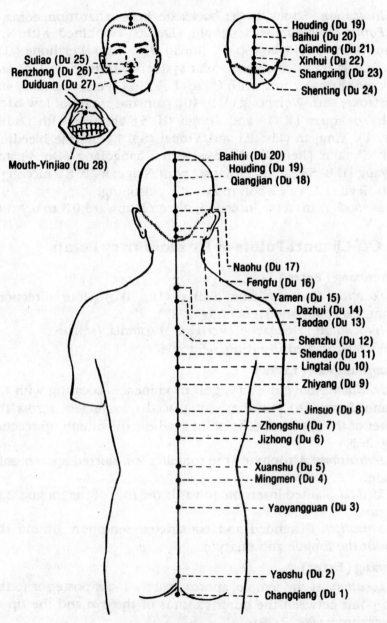

Suliao (Du 25)
Renzhong (Du 26)
Duiduan (Du 27)

Mouth-Yinjiao (Du 28)

Houding (Du 19)
Baihui (Du 20)
Qianding (Du 21)
Xinhui (Du 22)
Shangxing (Du 23)

Shenting (Du 24)

Baihui (Du 20)
Houding (Du 19)
Qiangjian (Du 18)

Naohu (Du 17)
Fengfu (Du 16)
Yamen (Du 15)
Dazhui (Du 14)
Taodao (Du 13)
Shenzhu (Du 12)
Shendao (Du 11)
Lingtai (Du 10)
Zhiyang (Du 9)
Jinsuo (Du 8)
Zhongshu (Du 7)
Jizhong (Du 6)
Xuanshu (Du 5)
Mingmen (Du 4)
Yaoyangguan (Du 3)
Yaoshu (Du 2)
Changqiang (Du 1)

Fig. 2-26. The Du Channel.

Indications: Shock, lower backache, heat exhaustion, coma.

Points combination: Renzhong (Du 26) combined with Nei-guan (P. 6), Sanyinjiao (Sp. 6), Jiquan (H. 1) and Weizhong (U.B. 40): disorders of cerebrovascular system; with Hegu (L.I. 4) and Shixuan (Extra): coma; with Quze (P. 3) and Weizhong (U.B. 40): sunstroke; with Weizhong (U.B. 40): pain and sprain of low back; with Yongquan (K. 1) and Tongli (H. 5): aphasia; with Dadun (Liv. 1), Xingjian (Liv. 2) and Yinbai (Sp. 1): uterine bleeding; with Shuifen (Ren 9): diuresi; with Changqiang (Du 1) and Feiyang (U.B. 58): anus prolapse; with Neiguan (P. 6): hiccough; with Hegu (L.I. 4): carbon monoxide poisoning.

Method: Transverse insertion, directed upward 0.3 to 0.9 *cun*.

15. Off-Channel Points or Extraordinary Points

Sishencong (Extra)

Location: One *cun* from Baihui (Du 20) in four directions (front, back, left and right) (*Fig.* 2-27).

Indications: Headache, vertigo, insomnia, seizure.

Method: Slanted insertion, 0.5 to 0.8 *cun*.

Shanglianquan (Extra)

Location: Above the laryngeal prominence. Locating with the thumb downward and the joint placed transversely across the center of the jaw bone. The point is where the thumb tip reaches (*Fig.* 2-28).

Indications: Atrophy of the tongue root, slurred speech, salivation.

Method: Slanted insertion, towards the root of the tongue, 2 to 3.5 *cun*.

Sensation: Distended and constricted sensation around the root or the tongue and pharynx.

Taiyang (Extra)

Location: At the temple, approximately 1 *cun* posterior to the mid-point between the outer canthus of the eye and the tip of the eyebrow (*Fig.* 2-29).

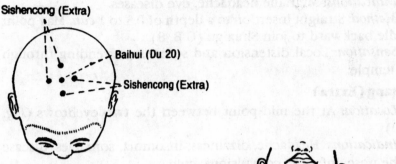

Fig. 2-27.

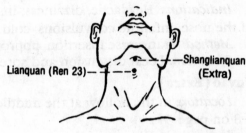

Fig. 2-29.

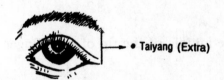

Fig. 2-28.

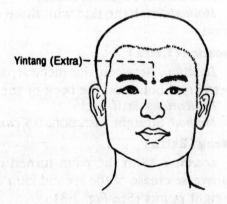

Fig. 2-30.

Indications: Migraine headache, eye diseases.

Method: Straight insertion to a depth of 0.5 to 1 *cun*. May point needle backward to join Shuaigu (G.B. 8).

Sensation: Local distension and soreness, extending through the temple.

Yintang (Extra)

Location: At the mid-point between the two eyebrows (*Fig.* 2-30).

Indications: Headache, dizziness, insomnia, sore eyes, disease of the nose, infantile convulsions, cold.

Method: Transverse insertion, approximately 0.2 to 0.5 *cun*.

Sensation: Local distension and soreness.

Yuyao (Extra)

Location: In the hollow at the middle of the eyebrow (See *Fig.* 2-8 on page 34).

Indications: Disease of the eye.

Method: Transverse insertion, direct needle towards either side about 0.2 to 0.8 *cun*.

Shixuan (Extra)

Location: Ten points, on the middle of the tip of each finger (*Fig.* 2-31).

Indications: Fainting, shock.

Method: Prick the skin with three-edged needle to draw a little blood.

Luozhen (Extra)

Location: Between the metacarpal joints of the 2nd and 3rd metacarpal bones on the back of the hand (*Fig.* 2-32).

Indications: Stiff neck.

Method: Straight insertion, 0.5 *cun*.

Sifeng (Extra)

Location: With the palm turned up, at the mid-point on the transverse crease of the second joint of the four fingers, altogether eight points (See *Fig.* 2-31).

Indications: Infantile indigestion, infantile night crying, hundred-day cough.

Method: Prick the skin, 0.1 *cun*, drawing a small amount of yellow fluid.

Shangbaxie (Extra)

Location: With the hand clenched, the point can be found in the small depression, 0.5 *cun* between the metacarpal joint of the back of hand (See *Fig*. 2-32).

Indications: Arthritic pain and swelling in finger joints, numbness, headache, toothache, sore throat.

Method: Insertion, 0.3-0.5 *cun*. Local needling sensation may extend towards the fingertips.

Bafeng (Extra)

Location: In the web between each of the toes, four on each foot, including Xingjian (Liv. 2), Neiting (St. 44) and Xiaxi (G.B. 43) (*Fig*. 2-33).

Indications: Pain in toes, beriberi.

Method: Slanted insertion, pointed upward 0.5-0.8 *cun*, or prick to draw a little blood.

Lanwei (Extra)

Location: Approximately 2 *cun* below Zusanli (St. 36) (See *Fig*. 2-9 on page 34).

Indications: Acute and chronic appendicitis.

Method: Straight insertion, 1-1.5 *cun*.

Xiyan (Extra)

Location: In the hollow on either side of the patellar tendon below the kneecap (See *Fig*. 2-9 on page 39).

Indications: Arthritic pain in knee.

Method: Slanted insertion, needle pointed towards opposite side, 1-2 *cun*, or join the other Xiyan (Extra).

Chuanxixue (Extra)

Location: 0.5 *cun* lateral to Dazhui (*Fig*. 2-34).

Indications: Bronchitis, cough.

Method: Slanted insertion, needle pointed slightly towards the spine, more than 1 *cun*. Needling sensation may extend down to back or lower back.

Huatuojiaji (Extra)

Location: Altogether 34 points distributed on both sides of the cervical, thoracic and lumbar vertebrae, 0.5 *cun* lateral to the medium line of the spine (*Fig*. 2-34).

Indications: Intercostal neuralgia, disease of spine.

Method: Straight insertion, 0.5 *cun*.

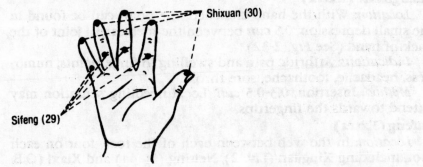

Fig. 2-31.

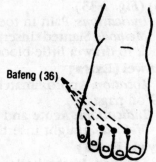

Fig. 2-33.

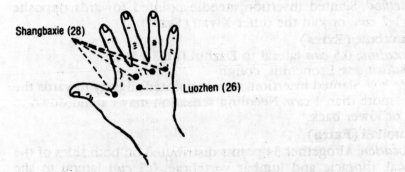

Fig. 2-32.

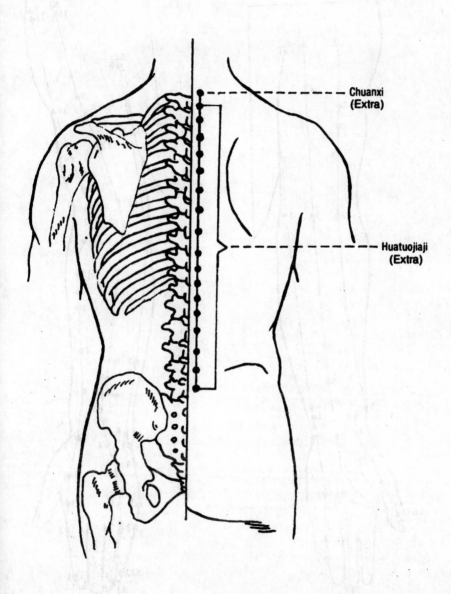

Chuanxi
(Extra)

Huatuojiaji
(Extra)

Fig. 2-34.

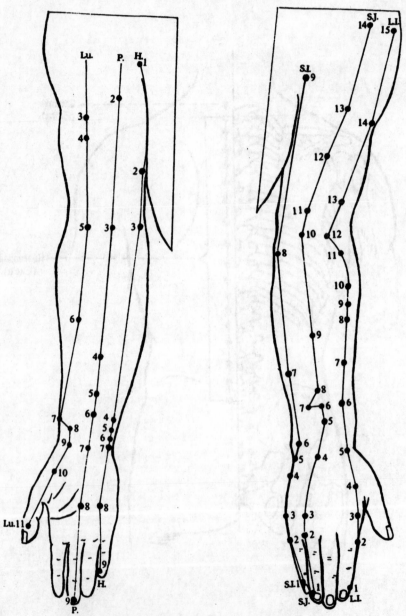

Fig. 2-35. The Points at the Upper Extremities.

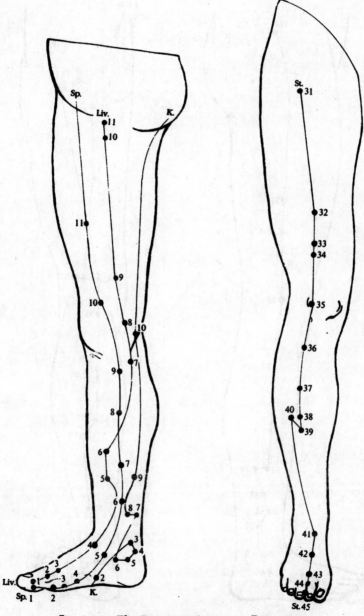

Fig. 2-36a. The Points at the Lower Extremities.

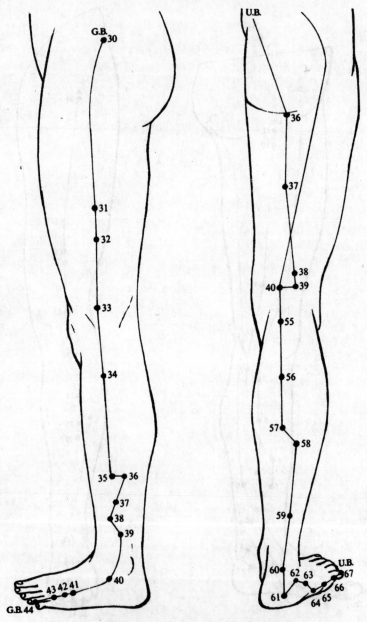

Fig. 2-36b. The Points at the Lower Extremities.

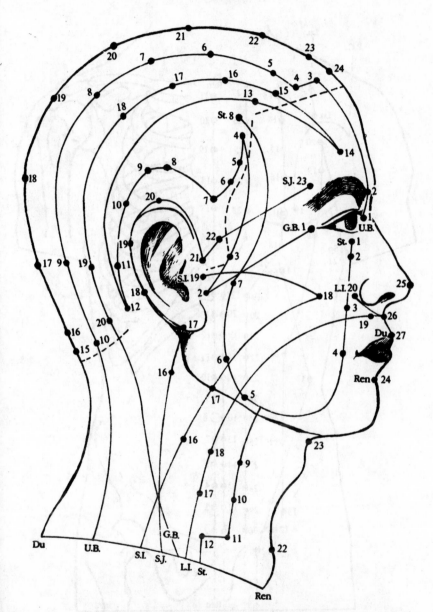

Fig. 2-37. The Points at the Head and Neck

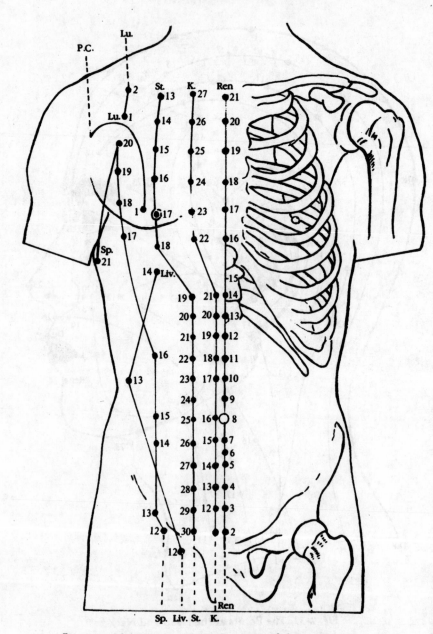

Fig. 2-38. The Points at the Chest and Abdominal Region.

106

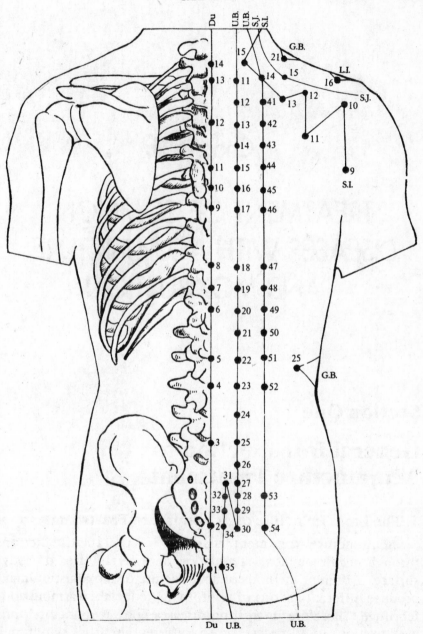

Fig. 2-39. The Points at the Back.

Chapter III

TREATMENT OF COMMON DISEASES WITH ACUPUNCTURE AND MOXIBUSTION

Section One

General Introduction to Acupuncture Treatment

1. The Basic Principle of Acupuncture Treatment

Acupuncture treatment displays its therapeutic action through needle or moxa stimulation on a certain area of body surface. Different methods of acupuncture or moxibustion may produce different actions of reinforcing, reducing, warming and febrifuge. Therefore in treating diseases with acupuncture and moxibustion it is necessary to differentiate the symptom-complex according to the basic theory of traditional Chinese

108

medicine, i.e. readjustment of the Yin and Yang imbalance according to the principles of "reinforcing the deficiency," "reducing the excess," "warming the coldness," and "clearing heat." These principles were described in *Neijing* (Canon of Yellow Emperor's Internal Medicine), a collection of ancient medical treatises which took shape 2,000 years ago. It says: "Reduce the excess, reinforce deficiency, dispel heat by rapid manipulation of needle, and disperse cold by retaining the needle," and "elevate the sinking of Qi by moxibustion," "remove blood stagnation by blood-letting method." These principles are still guiding our clinical practice now. "Reduce the excess" indicates that the reducing method of acupuncture treatment can be applied to the diseases and symptoms with hyperactivity of pathogenic factors. "Reinforce deficiency" means that the reinforcing method of acupuncture treatment is suitable for the diseases and symptoms with insufficiency of Zhengqi (body resistance). "Dispel heat by rapid manipulation" means that rapid withdrawal of needles without retention, or pricking with three-edged needle to let blood out are used for heat-natured symptom-complex. "Disperse cold by retaining the needle" means that a patient with Yang Xu (deficiency) and with a hyperactivity of pathogenic cold should not have strong acupuncture sensation, but the needles should be retained to wait for the coming of Qi. "Remove the blood stagnation by blood-letting method" indicates that diseases caused by blood stagnation should be treated by the pricking method to let the blood out. "Elevate the sinking of Qi by moxibustion" means that the diseases caused by deficiency or sinking of Qi, such as chronic dysentery or sudden prostration of Yang Qi with cold extremities and excessive sweating, should be treated by moxibustion.

2. The Principles of Selecting Points

The effect of acupuncture treatment does not only relate to the method of stimulation, but also closely to correctly identifying the point of stimulation. Generally different acupuncture points possess different indications. So the correct selection of acupuncture points directly acts upon the therapeutic effect and has very important clinical significance. It is said in *Neijing*: "Where the channels and collaterals pass by, there would be the indications of treatment for the associated diseases and symptoms." The basic principle is to select points according to the course of the channel, the distribution of points, and their indications. In clinical practice there are three ways for selecting points: local selection, distal selection and symptomatic selection.

Local Selection

This method selects the points on the disease location or near the affected site. For example, Zhongwan (Ren 12) is chosen to treat gastric pain; Quchi (L.I. 11) and Shousanli (L.I. 10) to treat elbow pain; Xiyan (Extra) and Yanglingquan (G.B. 34) are used to treat knee joint pain; Yangchi (S.J. 4) and Waiguan (S.J. 5) for wrist pain; Xiaguan (St. 7) and Jiache (St. 6) for toothache; Jingming (U.B. 1) and Sibai (St. 2) to treat eye diseases; Tinggong (S.I. 19) and Yifeng (S.J. 17) to treat deafness; Yingxiang (L.I. 20) and Yintang (Extra) for nose troubles; Tianshu (St. 25) and Daheng (Sp. 15) are selected for abdominal pain; etc.

Distal Selection

Points which are distal to the diseased area are selected according to the course of the channels. For instance, Zusanli (St. 36) is chosen to treat abdominal pain; Yanglingquan (G.B. 34) to treat hypochondriac pain; Hegu (L.I. 4) is used for toothache; Houxi (S.I. 3) for neck pain; Taichong (Liv. 3) for vertex headache; Shaoshang (Lu. 11) for sore throat; etc.

Symptomatic Selection

The selection of local and distal points are determined by the distance from point to the diseased area. Generally any illness or pain must be manifested by local pathological symptom or sign. As for some general diseases, or the patients without local pathological changes, points should be selected according to the symptom-complex of the disease. For example, Geshu (U.B. 17) is a specific point for the general condition of blood diseases;

Shanzhong (Ren 17) for the general condition of Qi problems; Taiyuan (Lu. 9) for vessel diseases; Yanglingquan (G.B. 34) for disorders of tendons; Dashu (U.B. 11) for problems of marrow; Zhangmen (Liv. 13) for diseases of Zang organs; Zhongwan (Ren 12) for disorders of Fu organs. These points have close relations with the disorders of Qi, blood, tendon, vessel, bone, marrow, Zang and Fu organs, so any disease or symptom of these eight aspects should be treated by the above corresponding points.

In addition, clinical experiences have proved that some points have a very good effect on certain kinds of diseases. But they cannot be selected according to the above-mentioned three principles. They are named as empirical points. Different doctors may have their own experienced points. For example, Xiaguan (St. 7) can be used for heel pain; Quchi (L.I. 11) for knee joints pain; Yangchi (S.J. 4) for ankle pain; etc.

The above methods of selecting points may be used separately or in combination. (Table 3-1)

3. The Basic Principles of Prescription and Combination of Points

In addition to the methods of individual point selection outlined above, there are several traditional methods of combining one or two points with others in an acupuncture prescription on the basis of their coordinated action. These techniques are flexible, permitting many variations according to the particular needs of the case. They are described as below:

Combining Upper Points with Lower Points

"Upper" refers to points on the arms and above the waist, "lower" to points on the legs and below the waist. This is the method of point combination most commonly practiced in the acupuncture clinic. For example, in the case of stomach disease, Neiguan (P. 6) on the upper limb may be combined extremely for sore throat or toothache Hegu (L.I. 4) on the hand can be combined with Neiting (St. 44) on the foot. For constipation, the Zhigou (S.J. 6) point on the forearm may be used together with

111

Table 3-1 **Examples for Selecting Points**

Disease Location	Distal Points	Local Points
Vertex	Taichong (Liv. 3)	Baihui (Du 20)
		Sishencong (Extra)
		Shangxing (Du 23)
Temple	Hand-Zhongzhu (S.J. 3)	Taiyang (Extra)
	Foot-Linqi (G.B. 41)	Shuaigu (G.B. 8)
	Xiaxi (G.B. 43)	
	Waiguan (S.J. 5)	
Forehead	Hegu (L.I. 4)	Yintang (Extra)
	Neiting (St. 44)	Yangbai (G.B. 14)
Nape	Houxi (S.I. 3)	Fengchi (G.B. 20)
	Lieque (Lu. 7)	Tianzhu (U.B. 10)
	Shugu (U.B. 65)	
Eye	Yanglao (S.I. 6)	Shangxing (Du 23)
	Guangming (G.B. 37)	Jingming (U.B. 1)
	Hegu (L.I. 4)	Chengqi (St. 1)
Nose	Quchi (L.I. 11)	Yintang (Extra)
	Hegu (L.I. 4)	Yingxiang (L.I. 20)
	Lidui (St. 45)	
Mouth & teeth	Hegu (L.I. 4)	Jiache (St. 6)
	Neiting (St. 44)	Xiaguan (St. 7)
		Dicang (St. 4)
Ear	Waiguan (S.J. 5)	Yifeng (S.J. 17)
	Hand-Zhongzhu (S.J. 3)	Tinggong (S.I. 19)
		Tinghui (G.B. 2)
		Ermen (S.J. 21)
Chest	Lieque (Lu. 7)	Tiantu (Ren 22)
	Chize (Lu. 5)	Feishu (U.B. 13)
	Neiguan (P. 6)	Shanzhong (Ren 17)
Throat	Shaoshang (Lu. 11)	Tiantu (Ren 22)
	Zhaohai (K. 6)	Lianquan (Ren 23)
Costal and hypochon-driac regions	Zhigou (S.J. 6)	Ganshu (U.B. 18)
	Yanglingquan (G.B. 34)	Qimen (Liv. 14)
		Wushu (G.B. 27)
Upper abdomen	Neiguan (P. 6)	Zhongwan (Ren 12)
	Zusanli (St. 36)	Weishu (U.B. 21)

112

Table 3-1 Examples for Selecting Points

(*Continued*)

Disease Location	Distal Points	Local Points
Lower abdomen	Sanyinjiao (Sp. 6)	Guanyuan (Ren 4)
	Yinbai (Sp. 1)	Qihai (Ren 6)
	Zhiyin (U.B. 67)	Tianshu (St. 25)
Lumbar region	Weizhong (U.B. 40)	Shenshu (U.B. 23)
	Yanglao (S.I. 6)	Dachangshu (U.B. 25)
	Renzhong (Du 26)	
Rectum	Chengshan (U.B. 57)	Changqiang (Du 1)
		Baihuanshu (U.B. 30)
Genital organ	Sanyinjiao (Sp. 6)	Zhongji (Ren 3)
		Guanyuan (Ren 4)
		Qugu (Ren 2)
Upper extremity	Huatuo Jiaji (Extra)	Jianyu (L.I. 15)
	(C.V.5—T.V.1)	Quchi (L.I. 11)
		Hegu (L.I. 4)
Lower extremity	Huatuo Jiaji (Extra)	Huantiao (G.B. 30)
	(L.V.3—S.V.1)	Weizhong (U.B. 40)
		Yanglingquan (G.B. 34)

Zusanli (St. 36) on the lower leg. For prolapse of uterus or rectum, Baihui (Du 20) on the top of head can be prescribed together with Zhaohai (K. 6) on the foot.

Combining Local with Distal Points

This technique combines local points with distant points (see Table 3-1).

Combining Points on the Front with Points on the Back

The "front" refers to the chest and abdomen, the "back" to the upper back and lumbar regions, points on both the front and back appropriate to a particular disease can be used in combination. This method is similar to the combination of Back-Shu Points with Front-Mu Points. But the points used in this method are more than these two points. For example, in the case of stomach disease, both Zhongwan (Ren 12) on the abdomen and Weishu (U.B. 21) on the back could be needled in tandem; or both Liangmen (St. 21) on the abdomen and Weicang (U.B. 50) on the chest and Xinshu (U.B. 15) on the back can be combined.

Combining Points on the Left Side with Points on the Right

Because of the symmetrical distribution and intersection of the channels, the points on the right side may be chosen to treat disease or pain on the left side of the body and vice versa. This is what the *Neijing* describes as "niu ci" (cross puncturing). For example, in the cases of hemiplegia, not only may a point on the affected side of the paralysis be selected, but also the same point on the healthy side may be used as well. For left shoulder pain, Yinlingquan (Sp. 9) of left temple, Yanglingquan (G.B. 34) and Xiaxi (G.B. 43) may be selected. In the cases of left facial paralysis, right Hegu (L.I. 4) can be chosen.

4. The Application of Specific Points

Specific points are the points of 14 regular channels which possess special properties and actions. They are mainly the Five Shu Points, Back-Shu and Front-Mu Points, Confluent Points of Eight Extra Channels, Eight Influential Points, Yuan-Source and Luo-Connecting Points, Xi-Cleft and Lower He-Sea Points. Clinically they can be selected singly or in combination with other points according to the above basic principle of selecting points.

The Yuan-Source Points and the Luo-Connecting Points

Each one of the Twelve Regular Channels has a Yuan-Source Point. In *Neijing* (Lingshu, Chapter 1 — Nine Needles and Twelve Yuan-Source Points), it says: "Those Twelve Yuan-Source Points are indicated for the diseases of five Zang and six Fu organs." So Yuan-Source Points are effective for diseases of internal organs. Luo-Connecting Points are the places where two exteriorly and interiorly related channels meet. The Luo-Connecting Points of Twelve Regular Channels are indicated by the symptoms of their respective "externally-internally related channels." Clinically, these two groups of points can be used separately or coordinately. When a channel is diseased, the Yuan-Source Point of its externally-internally related channel also can be used together with it to enhance the therapeutic effect. For instance, the Lung Channel of Hand-Taiyin and the Large Intestine Channel of Hand-Yangming are exteriorly-interiorly related. If the Lung Channel is involved, Taiyuan (Lu. 9), the Yuan-Source Point of the Lung Channel, and Pianli (L.I. 6), the Luo-Connecting Point of the Large Intestine Channel, may be prescribed. Or Hegu (L.I. 4), the Yuan-Source Point of the Large Intestine Channel, and Lieque (Lu. 7), the Luo-Connecting Point of the Large Intestine Channel, are selected to treat diseases of the Large Intestine Channel.

Table 3-2 The Yuan-Source and the Luo-Connecting Points

Channel	Yuan-Source Point	Luo-Connecting Point
Lung Channel of Hand-Taiyin	Taiyuan (Lu. 9)	Lieque (Lu. 7)
Pericardium Channel of Hand-Jueyin	Daling (P. 7)	Neiguan (P. 6)
Heart Channel of Hand-Shaoyin	Shenmen (H. 7)	Tongli (H. 5)
Spleen Channel of Foot-Taiyin	Taibai (Sp. 3)	Gongsun (Sp. 4)
Liver Channel of Foot-Jueyin	Taichong (Liv. 3)	Ligou (Liv. 5)
Kidney Channel of Foot-Shaoyin	Taixi (K. 3)	Dazhong (K. 4)
Large Intestine Channel of Hand-Yangming	Hegu (L.I. 4)	Pianli (L.I. 6)
Sanjiao Channel of Hand-Shaoyang	Yangchi (S.J. 4)	Waiguan (S.J. 5)
Small Intestine Channel of Hand-Taiyang	Hand-Wangu (S.I. 4)	Zhizheng (S.I. 7)
Stomach Channel of Foot-Yangming	Chongyang (St. 42)	Fenglong (St. 40)
Gall Bladder Channel of Foot-Shaoyang	Qiuxu (G.B. 40)	Guangming (G.B. 37)
Urinary Bladder Channel of Foot-Taiyang	Jinggu (U.B. 64)	Feiyang (U.B. 58)

The Back-Shu and the Front-Mu Points

Back-Shu Points are located on the back of the body where the Qi of Zang-Fu organs and channels of the back converge. Front-Mu Points are on the front of the body where the Qi of Zang-Fu organs and channels on the front concentrate. Each Zang or Fu organ has a Back-Shu Point and a Front-Mu Point. If there is an occurrence of pathological changes of any Zang or Fu organ, an abnormal sensation such as tenderness or a sensitive spot would appear on the corresponding Back-Shu or Front-Mu point. Therefore, whenever a Zang or Fu organ is diseased, then the Back-Shu and Front-Mu Points could be combined. The Back-Shu Points and the Front-Mu Points can be used separately or in combination. For instance, Weishu (U.B. 21) of the back and Zhongwan (Ren 12) of the abdomen may be selected for gastric disorders. Pangguangshu (U.B. 28) of the sacral region and Zhongji (Ren 3) of the lower abdomen are chosen for diseases of the urinary bladder.

Neijing says, "To treat the Yang aspect for diseases of Yin nature," while "to treat the Yin aspect for diseases of Yang nature." In the selection of points, the Back-Shu Points relate to Yang and can be used in treating Zang diseases as well as diseases of the sense organs which are related to their respective corresponding Zang organs. For example, since traditional Chinese medicine holds that the liver opens to the eye or that the eye is the window of the liver, Ganshu (U.B. 18), which is the Back-Shu Point of the liver, may be chosen to treat eye disorders, as the eye is the "window" of the liver (or "liver opens to the eye"). Shenshu (U.B. 23), the Back-Shu Point of the kidney, can be selected to treat deafness or other ear problems, as the ear is the "window of the kidney" (or "kidney opens to the ear"). The Front-Mu Points relate to Yin. Their therapeutic function is mainly in treating disorders of the Fu organs and local areas. For instance, for stomach diseases, Zhongwan (Ren 12), as the Front-Mu Point of stomach, can be chosen in the treatment. For disorders of Large Intestine Channel, Tianshu (St. 25), as the Front-Mu Point of Large Intestine Channel, may be used.

Table 3-3 The Back-Shu Points and the Front-Mu Points

Back-Shu Point	Zang-Fu organ	Front-Mu Point
Feishu (U.B. 13)	Lung	Zhongfu (Lu. 1)
Jueyinshu (U.B. 14)	Pericardium	Shanzhong (Ren 17)
Xinshu (U.B. 15)	Heart	Juque (Ren 14)
Ganshu (U.B. 18)	Liver	Qimen (Liv. 14)
Danshu (U.B. 19)	Gall Bladder	Riyue (G.B. 24)
Pishu (U.B. 20)	Spleen	Zhangmen (Liv. 13)
Weishu (U.B. 21)	Stomach	Zhongwan (Ren 12)
Sanjiaoshu (U.B. 22)	Sanjiao	Shimen (Ren 5)
Shenshu (U.B. 23)	Kidney	Jingmen (G.B. 25)
Dachangshu (U.B. 25)	Large Intestine	Tianshu (St. 25)
Xiaochangshu (U.B. 27)	Small Intestine	Guanyuan (Ren 4)
Pangguangshu (U.B. 28)	Urinary Bladder	Zhongji (Ren 3)

Five Shu Points

The Five Shu Points are respectively attributed to the Five Elements, and distributed below knees and elbows. They are the places where the Qi of channels is transferred. The order of the Five Elements in the Yin channels is Wood (Jing-Well), Fire (Rong-Spring), Earth (Shu-Stream), Metal (Jing-River), Water (He-Sea); the order in the Yang channels is Metal (Jing-Well), Water (Rong-Spring), Wood (Shu-Stream), Fire (Jing-River), Earth (He-Sea). According to the inter-generating relation of the Five Elements, each channel has a "mother point" and a "son point." Clinically acupuncture points not only can be selected according to the characteristics of the Five Shu Points, but also to the interrelationships of the Five Elements. For instance, the Liver Channel relates to Wood in Five Elements; therefore, in case of the Shi (Excess) and Heat symptom-complex of the Liver Channel, Xingjian (Liv. 2) can be chosen to reduce the excessive heat. Because Xingjian (Liv. 2) is the Rong-Spring (Fire) Point of the

Table 3-4 The Five Shu Points of the Yin Channels

Channel	Jing-Well (Wood)	Rong-Spring (Fire)	Shu-Stream (Earth)	Jing-River (Metal)	He-Sea (Water)
Lung Channel of Hand-Taiyin	Shaoshang (Lu. 11)	Yuji (Lu. 10)	Taiyuan (Lu. 9)	Jingqu (Lu. 8)	Chize (Lu. 5)
Pericardium Chan. of Hand-Shaoyin	Zhongchong (P. 9)	Laogong (P. 8)	Daling (P. 7)	Jianshi (P. 5)	Quze (P. 3)
Heart Channel of Hand-Shaoyin	Shaochong (H. 9)	Shaofu (H. 8)	Shenmen (H. 7)	Lingdao (H. 4)	Shaohai (H. 3)
Spleen Channel of Foot-Shaoyin	Yinbai (Sp. 1)	Dadu (Sp. 2)	Taibai (Sp. 3)	Shangqiu (Sp. 5)	Yinlingquan (Sp. 9)
Liver Channel of Foot-Jueyin	Dadun (Liv. 1)	Xingjian (Liv. 2)	Taichong (Liv. 3)	Zhongfeng (Liv. 4)	Ququan (Liv. 8)
Kidney Channel of Foot-Shaoyin	Yongquan (K. 1)	Rangu (K. 2)	Taixi (K. 3)	Fuliu (K. 7)	Yingu (K. 10)

Table 3-5 The Five Shu Points of the Yang Channels

Channel	Jing-Well (Metal)	Rong-Spring (Water)	Shu-Stream (Wood)	Jing-River (Fire)	He-Sea (Earth)
Large Intestine Chan. of Hand-Yangming	Shangyang (L.I. 1)	Erjian (L.I. 2)	Sanjian (L.I. 3)	Yangxi (L.I. 5)	Quchi (L.I. 11)
Sanjiao Channel of Hand-Shaoyang	Guanchong (S.J. 1)	Yemen (S.J. 2)	Hand-Zhongzhu (S.J. 3)	Zhigou (S.J. 6)	Tianjing (S.J. 10)
Small Intestine Channel of Hand-Shaoyang	Shaoze (S.I. 1)	Qiangu (S.I. 2)	Houxi (S.I. 3)	Yanggu (S.I. 5)	Xiaohai (S.I. 8)
Stomach Channel of Foot-Yangming	Lidui (St. 45)	Neiting (St. 44)	Xiangu (St. 43)	Jiexi (St. 41)	Zusanli (St. 36)
Gall Bladder Channel of Foot-Shaoyang	Foot-Qiaoyin (G.B.44)	Xiaxi (G.B. 43)	Foot-Linqi (G.B. 41)	Yangfu ·(G.B. 38)	Yanglingquan (G.B. 34)
Urinary Bladder Channel of Foot-Taiyang	Zhiyin (U.B. 67)	Foot-Tonggu (U.B. 66)	Shugu (U.B. 65)	Kunlun (U.B. 60)	Weizhong (U.B. 40)

Liver Channel, so this is to reduce the "son point." For Xu (deficiency) symptom-complex of Liver Channel, Ququan (Liv. 8) may be selected for the purposes of reinforcing. Because Ququan (Liv. 8) is the He-Sea (Water) Point of the Liver Channel, so this is to reinforce the "mother point" for the Xu symptom-complex.

The Xi-Cleft Points

The Xi-Cleft Points have the properties of treating acute diseases occurring in their respective related Zang-Fu organs. For instance, Kongzui (Lu. 6) of the Lung Channel of Hand-Taiyin is effective on hemoptysis; Wenliu (L.I. 7) of the Large Intestine Channel of Hand-Yangming is effective for borborygmus and abdominal pain; Liangqiu (St. 34) of the Stomach Channel of Foot-Yangming is for epigastric pain; Diji (Sp. 8) of the Spleen Channel of Foot-Taiyin is prescribed for menstrual pain.

Table 3-6 The Xi-Cleft Points

Channel	Xi-Cleft Point
Lung Channel of Hand-Taiyin	Kongzui (Lu. 6)
Pericardium Channel of Hand-Jueyin	Ximen (P. 4)
Heart Channel of Hand-Shaoyin	Yinxi (H. 6)
Large Intestine Channel of Hand-Yangming	Wenliu (L.I. 7)
Sanjiao Channel of Hand-Shaoyang	Huizong (S.J. 7)
Small Intestine Channel of Hand-Taiyang	Yanglao (S.I. 6)
Stomach Channel of Foot-Yangming	Liangqiu (St. 34)
Gall Bladder Channel of Foot-Shaoyang	Waiqiu (G.B. 36)
Urinary Bladder Channel of Foot-Taiyin	Jinmen (U.B. 63)
Spleen Channel of Foot-Taiyin	Diji (Sp. 8)
Liver Channel of Foot-Jueyin	Foot-Zhongdu (Liv. 6)
Kidney Channel of Foot-Shaoyin	Shuiquan (K. 5)
Yangqiao Channel	Fuyang (U.B. 59)
Yinqiao Channel	Jiaoxin (K. 8)
Yangwei Channel	Yangjiao (G.B. 35)
Yinwei Channel	Zhubin (K. 9)

The Eight Influential Points

There are Eight Influential Points, each of which has an effect on the diseases of certain body tissue. For instance, the Influential Point of the Zang organ, Zhangmen (Liv. 13), is chosen to treat weakness of the spleen; the Influential Point of the Fu organ, Zhongwan (Ren 12), for borborygmus, vomiting and diarrhea; the Influential Point of Qi, Shanzhong (Ren 17), is used for cough and asthma; the Influential Point of the blood, Geshu (U.B. 17), is used for hematemesis, wasting and consumptive diseases; the Influential Point of tendons and muscles, Yanglingquan (G.B. 34), is called on for muscular atrophy and weakness of the joints; the Influential Point of vessels and pulse, Taiyuan (Lu. 9), for weakness of pulse and deficiency of Qi; the Influential Point of bone, Dashu (U.B. 11), is chosen for painful joints and rheumatism; the Influential Point of the marrow, Xuanzhong (G.B. 39), is used for apoplexy, paralysis; etc.

Table 3-7 The Eight Influential Points

Influential Point of Zang organ	Zhangmen (Liv. 13)
Influential Point of Fu organ	Zhongwan (Ren 12)
Influential Point of Qi	Shanzhong (Ren 17)
Influential Point of blood	Geshu (U.B. 17)
Influential Point of tendon	Yanglingquan (G.B. 34)
Influential Point of vessels and pulse	Taiyuan (Lu. 9)
Influential Point of bone	Dashu (U.B. 11)
Influential Point of marrow	Xuanzhong (G.B. 39)

The Eight Confluent Points of Eight Extra Channels

The Eight Confluent Points are points in the extremities connecting the Eight Extra Channels and 12 regular channels. Gongsun (Sp. 4) connects with the Chong Channel; Neiguan (P. 6) connects with the Yinwei Channel; Houxi (S.I. 3) connects with the Du Channel; Shenmai (U.B. 62) connects with the Yangqiao Channel; Foot-Linqi (G.B. 41) connects with Dai Chan-

120

nel; Waiguan (S.J. 5) connects with the Yangwei Channel; Lieque (Lu. 7) connects with the Ren Channel; Zhaohai (K. 6) connects with the Yinqiao Channel. These points have the therapeutic properties for treating diseases of the extra channels and their related regular channels. Clinically, they may be used separately. For instance, if the Du Channel is affected, Houxi (S.I. 3) may be selected, and if the disease is related to the Chong Channel, Gongsun (Sp. 4) may be selected. Points of the upper extremities may at times be combined with those of the lower extremities. For example, Neiguan (P. 6), combined with Gongsun (Sp. 4), is indicated in diseases of the heart, chest and stomach. Houxi (S.I. 3), combined with Shenmai (U.B. 62), is indicated in diseases of

Table 3-8 The Eight Confluent Points of the Eight Confluent Point with Extra Channel

Extra Channels	Indication
Gongsun (Sp. 4) connecting with the Chong Channel	Disorder of heart, chest, stomach
Neiguan (P. 6) connecting with the Yinwei Channel	
Houxi (S.I. 3) connecting with the Du Channel	Disorders of neck, shoulder, back, inner canthus
Shenmai (U.B. 62) connecting with Yangqiao Channel	
Foot-Linqi (G.B. 41) connecting with the Dai Channel	Disorders of retroauricle, cheek, outer canthus
Waiguan (S.J. 5) connecting with the Yangwei Channel	
Lieque (Lu. 7) connecting with the Ren Channel	Disorder of throat, chest, lung
Zhaohai (K. 6) connecting with the Yinqiao Channel	

the neck, shoulder, back and inner canthus; Waiguan (S.J. 5), combined with Foot-Linqi (G.B. 41), is indicated for disorders of outer canthus, retroauricular region and cheek; Lieque (Lu. 7), combined with Zhaohai (K. 6), is indicated in disorders of the throat, chest and lung.

The Lower He-Sea Points

The six Fu organs are closely correlated with the three Yang channels of the foot. Each of the Fu organs has a Lower He-Sea Point along one of the Yang channels on the lower limb. At the same time, the three Yang channels of foot communicate with the three Yang channels of hand. The Lower He-Sea Points usually give satisfactory results in treating diseases of the six Fu organs. In treating diseases of the six Fu organs, the main points selected are the Lower He-Sea Points. For Instance, for gastric pain and acid regurgitation, Zusanli (St. 36) is chosen; for dysentery or appendicitis, Shangjuxu (St. 37) is used; Yanglingquan (G.B. 34) can be used for pain in gall bladder, vomiting, etc. According to what *Neijing* says, "He-Sea Points are used to treat disorders of Fu organs." The corresponding Lower He-Sea Points could be chosen to treat diseases of different Fu organs.

Table 3-9 The Lower He-Sea Points

Yang Channel of Hand	Taiyang—Xiajuxu (St. 39)
	Shaoyang—Weiyang (U.B. 39)
	Yangming—Shangjuxu (St. 37)
Yang Channel of Foot	Taiyang—Weizhong (U.B. 40)
	Shaoyang—Yanglingquan (G.B. 34)
	Yangming—Zusanli (St. 36)

Section Two

Acupuncture Treatment for Common Diseases and Symptoms

1. Wind-stroke

Wind-stroke is a commonly seen disease in the clinic occurring mostly among the elderly people. The causative factor of this disease is liver-Yang preponderance and liver-wind stirring resulting from emotional depression and anger due to disharmony of the Zang-Fu organs, Qi and blood causing imbalance of Yin and Yang, and dysfunction of the channels and collaterals. It can also be due to endogenous wind caused by phlegm-heat after over-indulgence of alcohol and fatty food. According to the depth of disease transmission, wind-stroke can be classified into "pathogenic wind attacking the channels," and "pathogenic wind attacking the Zang-Fu organs."

Differentiation

1. Pathogenic wind attacking the channels

Gradual in onset and with mild manifestations such as hemiplegia, numbness, deviated eyes and mouth, blurred speech due to stiffness of tongue, unconsciousness, sentimentality, yellow-sticky tongue-coating, wiry and forceful or slow and slippery pulse.

2. Pathogenic wind attacking the Zang-Fu organs

Acute in onset and with severe manifestations, such as collapse, unconsciousness, hemiplegia, salivation, aphagia and stiffness of the tongue. It can be divided further into "tense type," and "flaccid type" according to different causative factors and pathogenesis.

a. Tense type: It is mostly due to pervasive fire leading to an upward flow of the blood, liver-wind spreading and accumulation of phlemn. It is manifested by unclear mind, trismus, clenched fists, flushed face, coarse breathing, sputum rumbling in the throat, constipation and dysuria, slippery and rapid or wiry pulse.

b. Flaccid type: It is due to the declining of vitality and exhaustion of primary Yang manifested by lethargy, opened eyes and mouth, loose hands, enuresis, snoring with feeble breathing, cold extremities, thready and weak or deep pulse.

Treatment

1. Symptom-complex of "Pathogenic wind attacking the channels"

Method: To remove the obstruction of channels and regulate the circulation of Qi and blood by selecting the points of Yangming channels as the main points, and the points of Taiyang, Shaoyang and Jueyin channels as adjuvant points. Points of the affected side can be punctured with reducing method when the illness reaches the acute stage. The points of both sides can be used for chronic cases with the reinforcing method. Treatment is given once every other day. Retain the needle for 20-30 minutes. Ten treatments are considered as a course.

Prescription:

Hemiplegia: Jianyu (L.I. 15), Quchi (L.I. 11), Hegu (L.I. 4), Waiguan (S.J. 5), Huantiao (G.B. 30), Yanglingquan (G.B. 34), Zusanli (St. 36), Jiexi (St. 41), Kunlun (U.B. 60).

Secondary points selected alternatively or according to the symptoms:

Upper extremity: Jianliao (S.J. 14), Yangchi (S.J. 4). Houxi (S.I. 3) used alternatively.

Lower extremity: Fengshi (G.B. 31), Yinshi (St. 33), Xuanzhong (G.B. 39).

Contracture of elbow: Quze (P. 3).

Contracture of wrist: Daling (P. 7).

Contracture of knee: Ququan (Liv. 8).

Contracture of ankle: Taixi (K. 3).

Contracture of fingers: Baxie (Extra).

Contracture of toes: Bafeng (Extra).

Blurred Speech: Lianquan (Ren 23), Tongli (H. 5).

Deviated eyes and mouth: Dicang (St. 4), Jiache (St. 6), Hegu

(L.I. 4), Neiting (St. 44), Chengqi (St. 1), Yangbai (G.B. 14), Zanzhu (U.B. 2), Kunlun (U.B. 60), Yanglao (S.I. 6).

Salivation: Chengjiang (Ren 24).

2. Symptom-complex of "Pathogenic wind attacking the Zang-Fu organs"

a. Tense type

Method: To resuscitate and open the orifices by puncturing with reducing method or bleeding with three-edged needle at the points of Du channel and twelve Jing-Well points.

Prescription: Renzhong (Du 26), the twelve Jing-Well points, Taichong (Liv. 3), Fenglong (St. 40), Laogong (P. 8).

Trismus: Jiache (St. 6), Hegu (L.I. 4).

Dysphasia: Yamen (Du 15), Lianquan (Ren 23), Tongli (H. 5) Guanchong (S.J. 1).

b. Flaccid type

Method: Select the points of Ren channel as the main points and apply moxibustion with a large-sized moxa-cone.

Prescription: Guanyuan (Ren 4), Shenque (Ren 8) (indirect moxibustion with salt).

Remarks:

1. "Wind-stroke" described in this section corresponds to cerebral vascular accidents including cerebral hemorrhage, cerebral thrombosis, cerebral embolism, etc., and their sequelae.

2. At the acute stage of cerebrovascular accidents, emergency measures should be taken.

3. For the elderly people who have Qi-Deficiency or Liver-Yang preponderance manifested by the prodrome of dizziness, numbness of fingers or blurred speech care should be taken to avoid the onset of wind-stroke. A healthy life-style should be observed. Needling or moxibustion on the Fengshi (G.B. 31) and Zusanli (St. 36) points can be used to prevent wind-stroke.

2. Sunstroke

This is a kind of acute disease occurring in the summer. It is due to over-exposure to strong sunlight or staying in high temperature time. It mostly happens among pregnant women, elderly and weak people or patients with chronic diseases.

Sunstroke can be manifested in varying degrees of severity. Under the condition of high temperatures if the patient exhibits lassitude, weakness and numbness of four extremities, dizziness, stuffy chest, palpitation, unconcentrated mind, excessive perspiration, thirst, nausea, etc. This may suggest the prodrome of sunstroke. Timely supplementation of water and salt and rest in cool place may relieve the above symptoms. Sunstroke may be divided into mild and severe types.

Differentiation

Mild type: Aside from the above-mentioned prodrome of sunstroke, there can also be fever, flushed face, headache, irritability, fatigue, nausea and vomiting, pale complexion, thready and rapid pulse.

Severe type: Besides the above symptoms it is also accompanied by high fever, syncope or even coma and convulsion.

Treatment

1. Mild type

Method: To relieve exterior symptom-complex and clear up summer-heat, to harmonize the middle Jiao and remove summer-humidness by puncturing the points of Du channel, Yangming channels of hand and foot, and the pericardium channel with the reducing method.

Prescription: Dazhui (Du 14), Hegu (L.I. 4), Xiangu (St. 43), Neiguan (P. 6), Zusanli (St. 36).

Headache: Touwei (St. 8), Fengchi (G.B. 20), Taiyang (Extra).

Vomiting: Zhongwan (Ren 12).

2. Severe type

Method: To clear up summer-heat, tranquilize heart and open the orifice by puncturing the points of the Du, Foot-Taiyang and Hand-Jueyin channels with the reducing or blood-letting method.

Prescription: Baihui (Du 20), Renzhong (Du 26), Shixuan (Extra), Quchi (L.I. 11), Weizhong (U.B. 40), Quze (P. 3).

Convulsion: Yanglingquan (G.B. 34).

Cold extremity with sweating and feeble and forceless pulse: Guanyuan (Ren 4), Qihai (Ren 6), Taiyuan (Lu. 9), Yinxi (H. 6).

Remarks: Emergency measures should be taken for severe sunstroke. Place the patient in a cool and well ventilated place. If patient has high fever without perspiration but with pale complexion and cold limbs, should be rubbed on the body with warm water, or hot compresses applied on the Guanyuan (Ren 4) and Qihai (Ren 6).

3. Shock

Shock is due to a complex variety of causes. The main manifestations are pale complexion, cold and sweaty extremities, low blood pressure (in adults the systolic pressure is lower than 80 mm Hg, 25 percent lower than basic blood pressure), cyanosis, rapid and thready pulse, poor blood content of veins, decreased amount of urine, dull emotion, etc. These signs are caused by the absolute or relative decrease of effective circulatory blood, leading to insufficient blood in the tissues, In traditional Chinese medicine shock is classified under either "flaccid symptom-complex" or "syncopic symptom-complex."

Treatment

Main points: Renzhong (Du 26), Shenque (Ren 8), Baihui (Du 20), Suliao (Du 25).

Method: Firstly puncture Renzhong (Du 26), Zhongchong (P. 9) and Zusanli (St. 36) with intermittent manipulation of the needles once every 4-5 seconds. If there is no improvement after 3-5 minutes of stimulation, then Neiguan should be added. The other points can be selected according to different symptoms. For example, Baihui (Du 20) and Suliao (Du 25) are added to lower the blood pressure; moxibustion on Guanyuan (Ren 4), Shenque (Ren 8) and Zusanli (St. 36) for excessive sweating with cold limbs.

4. The Common Cold

Common cold is a disease frequently seen in the clinic caused by exogenous pathogenic factors which occur mostly in autumn and winter. It is also named "shangfeng" (injured by wind) in Chinese. Main symptoms are nasal obstruction, running nose, sneezing, sore throat, cough, headache, chills and fever. The severity of common cold is related to the strongness of Wei (defensive) Qi and to the depth of transmission of pathogenic factors. The causative factor of the common cold is pathogenic wind which combines with cold, heat, and summer humid-heat. Wind-cold type mostly occurs in autumn and winter, while wind-heat type mostly in spring and summer. Common cold caused by summer humid-heat often occurs in late summer.

Differentiation

1. Wind-cold type: Pathogenic wind-cold blocks in the exterior body because lung Qi fails to spread. Symptoms are discharge and obstruction, itching of throat, sneezing, cough, thin sputum, severe aversion to cold with mild fever, no sweating, general aching, headache, superficial and tense pulse, thin and white tongue coating.

2. Wind-heat type: Pathogenic wind-heat affects the lung which loses its function of descending the Qi. It is manifested by high fever with sweating and slight aversion to cold, cough with thick sputum, sore throat, thirst, dry nose, superficial and rapid pulse, thin and little yellow tongue coating.

3. Summer humid-heat type: Summer-humidness injures the exterior of body causing disharmony of lung and Wei (defensive) Qi. This is manifested by pain and distension of head. The feeling of "cloth wrapping around the head," general heaviness and aching of body, fever, aversion to cold with little sweating, mild cough with white and sticky sputum, stuffiness of chest, fullness of epigastric region, abdominal distension, loose stool, yellow and scanty urine, tastelessness in mouth with no thirst, preference for hot drinks, thick and sticky or yellow sticky tongue coating, slow or superficial and rapid pulse.

Treatment

1. Wind-cold type

128

Method: To expel pathogenic wind and disperse cold by puncturing the points of the Hand-Taiyin, Yangming and Foot-Taiyang channels with the reducing method; and moxibustion is applicable.

Prescription: Yingxiang (L.I. 20), Lieque (Lu. 7), Zhizheng (S.I. 7), Fengmen (U.B. 12), Fengchi (G.B. 20), Hegu (L.I. 4).

Headache: Yintang (Extra), Taiyang (Extra 2).

Sore aching back: Cupping on the Feishu (U.B. 13), or push cup from Dazhui (Du 14) downward to lumbar region, then push upward, and remove it after cupping at Feishu (U.B. 13) for 10-20 minutes.

2. Wind-heat type

Method: To disperse wind-heat and regulate circulation of lung Qi by selecting the points of Hand-Taiyin, Yangming and Shaoyang channels with reducing method of acupuncture or with blood-letting method of three-edged needle.

Prescription: Chize (Lu. 5), Yuji (Lu. 10), Quchi (L.I. 11), Neiting (St. 44), Dazhui (Du 14), Waiguan (S.J. 5).

Soreness and swelling of throat: Shaoshang (Lu. 11). Prick with three-edged needle to let the blood out.

Infantile high fever: Renzhong (Du 26), Shixuan (Extra).

3. Summer humid-heat type

Method: To clear up summer-heat and remove summer-humidness from the exterior by puncturing the points of the Taiyin, Yangming and Sanjiao channels with the reducing method.

Prescription: Kongzui (Lu. 6), Hegu (L.I. 4), Zhongwan (Ren 12), Zusanli (St. 36), Zhigou (S.J. 6).

High fever: Dazhui (Du 14).

Excessive humidness: Yinlingquan (Sp. 9).

Abdominal distension and loose stool: Tianshu (St. 25).

Yang-Deficiency and Qi-Deficiency: Zusanli (St. 36), Gaohuangshu (U.B. 43) with moxibustion.

Yin-deficiency and blood-deficiency: Feishu (U.B. 13), Xuehai (Sp. 10), Fuliu (K. 7) with the reinforcing method of acupuncture.

Remarks:

1. The symptoms of common cold are similar to the symp-

toms of some infectious diseases, so clinical differentiation should be done between them.

2. Someone reported that acupuncture was applied to prevent influenza among 818 healthy subjects.

Method: Punctured Zusanli (St. 36) of one side with the reinforcing method, withdrew the needle until there was the sensation of distension, soreness or tingling at the dorsum of foot. Each subject had one acupuncture treatment with one needle. There was not a single case of influenza after the preventive acupuncture. It shows that acupuncture is an effective means to prevent influenza.

3. Report: Acupuncture treatment for 373 cases of influenza.
Points: Dazhui (Du 14), Hegu (L.I. 4), Zusanli (St. 36).
Method: Strong stimulation, on retention of needles.

Effect: 198 among 373 cases had the fever lowered 24 hours after acupuncture (53.08 percent). In 51 cases, those who had no fever had follow-up together with the rest of the cases. It showed that the other symptoms were eliminated and the patients went back to their working post.

5. Sore Throat

Sore throat is mostly caused by acute tonsillitis and pharyngitis. Clinical manifestations are redness, swelling and pain of the throat or the general symptoms of aversion to cold and fever. Traditional Chinese medicine considers this is due to the accumulation of wind-heat and toxic fire in the upper Jiao. Acupuncture provides excellent results in relieving pain.

Treatment

Main points: Shaoshang (Lu. 11), Hegu (L.I. 4).

Combined points: Neiting (St. 44), Quchi (L.I. 11), Tiantu (Ren 22), Chize (Lu. 5).

Method: Prick Shaoshang (Lu. 11) with a three-edged needle to let the blood out. Generally pain can be stopped in a few minutes. Puncturing Quchi (L.I. 11) can be added for fever; Tiantu (Ren 22) and Chize (Lu. 5) for excessive sputum.

Typical case: Female, 40 years of age.

"She came to see the doctor two days after she got a common cold, complicated with a sore throat. We did blood-letting with a three-edged needle on Shaoshang (Lu. 11), and punctured Hegu (L.I. 4) of both sides with filiform needle. Soon after the pricking on Shaoshang (Lu. 11) pain was obviously relieved. After puncturing Hegu (L.I. 4), pain was basically stopped."

6. Chronic Pharyngolaryngitis

Chronic pharyngolaryngitis is caused by untimely treatment or recurrence at the acute stage. Patient feels discomfort, dryness, itching or clogged throat accompanied by hoarseness of voice. It is difficult to cure, often lasting for several months or years, repeated onsets may aggravate the disease condition. Acupuncture is very effective in relieving the symptoms.

Treatment

Main points: Lianquan (Ren 23), Quchi (L.I. 11), Chize (Lu. 5), Taiyuan (Lu. 9).

Combined points: Hegu (L.I. 4), Tiantu (Ren 22), Shaoshang (Lu. 11), Zhongchong (P. 9), Renying (St. 9).

Method: Those patients with dryness and itching as the main symptoms can first be treated by puncturing Lianquan (Ren 23), Taiyuan (Lu. 9), Chize (Lu. 5) and Quchi (L.I. 11). Puncture Renying (St. 9) and Tiantu (Ren 22) for the patients who have the feeling of something foreign in the throat. Blood-letting with a three-edged needle on Shaoshang (Lu. 11) and Zhongchong (P. 9) is used for severe sore throat.

Typical case: Female, 30 years of age.

"She came to our clinic because of dryness and itching of the throat. She also complained that she had got chronic laryngitis for several years, and had been treated by drug administration of traditional Chinese medicine and Western medicine with poor results. Then we gave her acupuncture treatment on Taiyuan (Lu. 9), Chize (Lu. 5) and Quchi (L.I. 11) of both sides. During the retention of needles, the patient felt that the fluid was permeating through the throat. The symptoms of throat dryness and itching disappeared soon after the acupuncture treatment."

7. Asthma

Asthma is a common and recurrent disorder of the respiratory system. Asthma in Chinese is "xiaochuan." "Xiao" and "chuan" are differentiated by different symptoms. "Chuan" indicates dyspnea. "Xiao" indicates sputum gurgling in the throat. Because "xiao" and "chuan" have similar etiology and pathogenesis, so they are always described together in one name, "xiaochuan" and translated as asthma.

The causative factor of this disease is due to invasion of exogenous pathogenic wind-cold or wind-heat, and the smelling of paint, smoke or pollens; or due to emotional disturbance or overstrain leading to the affection of the lung. The lung loses its function of spreading lung-Qi thereby causing accumulation of phlegm humor, which obstructs the respiratory tract; or due to an over-intake of cold, sour, fatty food, fish or shrimps and the spleen fails to carry on its function of transportation and transformation so that it also produces phlegm-humor stagnation in the lung. Asthma results from an obstruction of the respiratory tract. At the acute stage, it is mostly a Shi (excess) condition; after repeated occurrence it becomes a Xu (deficiency) type.

Differentiation

1. Shi type

It occurs mostly in winter due to an invasion of exogenous pathogenic wind-cold, causing the cold-humor accumulation in the lung and obstruction in the respiratory tract. Manifestations are dyspnea, wheezing noises, cough with little white and thin sputum or with foamy sputum expelled with difficulty, fear of cold, little or no sweating, and headaches and general aching, white and slippery tongue coating, tense or superficial-tense pulse. If exogenous pathogenic wind-cold causes heat to accumulate in the lung so that it loses its function of descending Qi, the symptoms would be cough and asthma with coarse breathing, flushed face, fever with sweating, yellow-sticky sputum which is difficult to expel, thirst, irritability, pain in the chest due to cough, yellow-sticky tongue coating, superficial-forceful or slippery-rapid pulse.

2. Xu type

Xu (deficiency) of the lung is manifested by pale and luster-less complexion, spontaneous sweating with aversion to cold, shortness and weakness of breathing, weakness of speaking, nasal obstruction, sneezing, fatigue, light red tongue proper, thready, rapid and forceless pulse. If it is due to spleen Xu (deficiency), symptoms would be lusterless complexion, poor appetite, fullness of epigastric region, excessive sputum, general fatigue, loose stool or diarrhea, flabby tongue body with thick-sticky coating, slow-slippery or soft-slow pulse. If it is due to kidney Xu (deficiency), symptoms would be accompanied by a dark complexion, hasty breathing which is exacerbated by movement, palpitation, dizziness, ringing in the ears, sore aching of the low back, cold lower extremities, pale tongue proper, deep, thready and forceless pulse. If it is due to heart Qi Xu (deficiency) and enervated heart Yang, it would be also accompanied by palpitation, excessive sweating, blurred mind, blue lips and nails, cold extremities, purple spots on tongue surface, with feeble or intermittent pulse.

Treatment

1. Shi type

Method: To disperse pathogenic cold, spread lung Qi and soothe asthma by selecting the points of the Hand-Taiyin and Foot-Taiyang channels with the reducing method or with moxibustion on points of back or with fire-cupping for wind-cold type illnesses. Points of the Foot-Yangming channel are used for the phlegm-heat type with no moxibustion method.

Prescription: Shanzhong (Ren 17), Lieque (Lu. 7), Feishu (U.B. 13), Chize (Lu. 5).

Wind-cold: Fengmen (U.B. 12).

Phlegm-heat: Fenglong (St. 40), Dazhui (Du 14), Kongzui (Lu. 6)

Severe asthma: Tiantu (Ren 22), Dingchuan (Extra, 1.5 *cun* bilateral to Dazhui, Du 14) or cupping on Feishu (U.B. 13) and Yunmen (Lu. 2).

2. Xu type

Method: To support the Zheng Qi (body resistance) and culti- vate the foundation of essential Qi, i.e. to reinforce the lung and kidney Qi by the reinforcing method or moxibustion.

Prescription: Feishu (U.B. 13), Gaohuangshu (U.B. 43), Qihai (Ren 6), Shenshu (U.B. 23), Zusanli (St. 36), Taiyuan (Lu. 9), Taixi (K. 3).

Remarks:

1. Asthma here includes bronchial asthma, asthmatic bronchi- tis, and dyspnea in some other lung diseases.

2. If asthma is accompanied by bronchitis, it should be treated soon after the relief of asthma.

3. Severe onset of asthma or those who have had long time recurrence of asthma should be treated together with drugs.

4. Preventive measures should be considered before the onset of asthma. For example, put on more clothes when the weather becomes colder. People with allergic body constitution should avoid contact with allergens or sensitive food.

5. It is reported that the acupuncture effect on asthma is realized through the action of anti-inflammation and promotion of absorbing inflammative exudate. Clinical practice has proved that acupuncture has absorptive effect on pulmonary inflamma- tion.

8. Headache

Headache is a common symptom in the clinic which is seen among various acute and chronic diseases. This section mainly discusses the headache caused by "wind attacking the channels" or liver-Yang preponderance, or deficiency of Qi and blood. If it is a complicated symptom of other diseases, it will not be des- cribed here.

Differentiation

1. "Wind attacking channels" type

Due to an invasion by exogenous pathogenic wind, cold and damp stagnating in the channels of the head region, it causes headache because of obstruction of Qi and blood circulation. Symptoms are intermittent and localized pricking pain, or distension and throbbing pain with lumps on the scalp, nasal obstruction and discharge, white tongue coating, wiry and tense pulse. In severe cases, it is complicated with nausea, vomiting, dizziness and vertigo, perspiration and pale complexion.

2. Liver-Yang preponderance type

It is due to emotional depression and anger bringing about Qi stagnation which changes into fire, further leading to liver-Yang preponderance or it is due to kidney-Yin exhaustion causing liver-Yang and liver-wind flowing upward. They are manifested by spasmodic pain at the corner of the head, or over the whole temporal region, irritability and readiness to anger, flushed face and bitter taste in the mouth, wiry and rapid pulse, red tongue proper with yellow coating.

3. Phlegm-humor type

The patient's body is constitutionally fat. This combined with over-indulgence in sweet and fatty food produces excessive pathogenic damp which obstructs the channels. It is manifested by blunt pain, like a cloth wrapped around the head, stuffiness and fullness of the chest and epigastric regions, nausea, vomiting with mucus, loose stool, white sticky tongue coating and slippery pulse.

4. Deficiency of Qi and blood type

It is due to weakness of the body after prolonged chronic disease or serious hemorrhage causing deficiency. Blood fails to flow up to nourish the brain marrow. Due to blood deficiency, the channels in the head region become empty and this leads to the following. Its symptoms: dizziness and headache, continuous and dull pain, general fatigue, palpitation, lusterless complexion, preference for warmth, fear for cold, pale tongue proper with thin and white coating, thready and weak pulse.

Treatment

1. "Wind attacking channels" type

Method: To disperse wind and cold and remove obstruction of channels by selecting the points of Shaoyang channels of hand and foot, and Yangming channels with the reducing method of acupuncture.

Prescription: Fengchi (G.B. 20), Touwei (St. 8), Tongtian (U.B. 7), Hegu (L.I. 4), Sanyangluo (S.J. 8).

Points added according to the symptoms:

Frontal headache: Shangxing (Du 23), Yangbai (G.B. 14);

Vertex headache: Baihui (Du 20), Qianding (Du 21);

Occipital headache: Tianzhu (U.B. 10), Houding (Du 19);

Temporal headache: Shuaigu (G.B. 8), Taiyang (Extra).

2. Liver-Yang preponderance type

Method: To pacify liver-Yang and subdue liver-wind by puncturing the points of Shaoyang, Jueyin and Shaoyin channels of foot with the reducing method.

Prescription: Xuanlu (G.B. 5), Hanyan (G.B. 4), Taichong (Liv. 3), Taixi (K. 3).

Redness of eyes: Bleeding on the Guanchong (S.J. 1).

Hotness of face: Neiting (St. 44).

3. Phlegm-humor type

Method: To resolve phlegm-humor, remove obstruction of channels and stop pain by puncturing the points of Ren, Du and Foot-Yangming channels with the reducing method.

Prescription: Zhongwan (Ren 12), Fenglong (St. 40), Baihui (Du 20), Yintang (Extra).

Points added according to the symptoms:

Vomiting: Neiguan (P. 6).

Loose stool: Tianshu (St. 25).

4. Deficiency of Qi and blood:

Method: To nourish Qi and blood, regulate the circulation of Qi and blood and to stop pain by puncturing the points of Du, Foot-Yangming and Taiyang channels with reinforcing method.

Prescription: Shangxing (Du 23), Xuehai (Sp. 10), Zusanli (St. 36), Sanyinjiao (Sp. 6). After the relief of headache, moxibustion is advisable on Ganshu (U.B. 18), Pishu (U.B. 20), Shenshu (U.B. 23), and Qihai (Ren 6).

Remarks:

1. Headache is often seen in the diseases like hypertension, intracranial tumor, neural functional headache, migraine or infectious febrile diseases, etc.

2. If the headache has been treated many times by acupuncture showing no improvement but perhaps aggravation, the examination should be made to find out the primary disease and give consideration of cranial pathological changes.

3. Reference: Acupuncture treatment was applied in 73 cases of neural headache by using the method of combination of local points with distal points. After treatment, it showed that 18 cases were cured (the average treatment was 9.3 times); 28 cases had remarkable defectiveness (average treatment 8.4 times); 23 cases improved (average treatment 7.6 times); 2 cases had no result (average treatment 7.5 times). Two cases were not included in the statistics. So the effective rate was 94.52 percent. The curative rate was 64.8 percent.

9. Toothache

Toothache is very common and is generally caused by pulpitis, periodontitis, pericoronitis and dental caries. Traditional Chinese medicine holds that toothache can be divided into Xu and Shi types. Xu (deficiency) type is caused by kidney-Yin deficiency leading fire to flare up. Shi (excess) type is caused by the accumulation of stomach-heat and further invasion of exogenous wind-heat which is also called "wind-fire toothache."

Xu-fire toothache is manifested by pain, loose teeth, neither tends nor swelling of gums, dry throat without thirst, red tongue proper with thin coating and thready pulse.

Shi-fire toothache is characterized by pain, redness and swelling of gums, thirst with preference of cold drinks, foul smell of mouth, constipation, yellow urine, yellow tongue coating and rapid pulse.

Treatment

Main points: Yatong (Extra, in the palm between the 3rd and

the 4th metacarpal bones, 1 *cun* proximal to metacarpo-
phalangeal crease) and Hegu (L.I. 4) can be used for toothache
caused by various reasons. Puncture firstly Hegu (L.I. 4) with the
reducing method of rotating the needle and Yatong (Extra) with
manipulation of vibrating the needle. The pain may be stopped
after 2-5 minutes of needling manipulation. If there is not much
improvement some other points can be added; for instance,
Xiaguan (St. 7) is added for upper toothache; Jiache (St. 6) for
lower toothache; Zhaohai (K. 6), Taixi (K. 3), Xingjian (Liv. 2) and
Taichong (Liv. 3) for "Kidney-Xu toothache"; Waiguan (S.J. 5)
and Neiting (St. 44) for "wind-fire toothache."

Typical case: Female, 60 years of age.

"She came to the hospital on July 2, 1985 for she had had a
toothache on the left side for two weeks. She complained that she
began to have the toothache two weeks ago with the pain
aggravated for the last few days. The acute pain had disturbed
her sleep. The dentist diagnosed it as dentes caviosus. She was
given oral administration of ante-inflammation drugs and pain-
killers, showing poor results. Acupuncture treatment was applied
to the points Taichong (Liv. 3), Neiting (St. 44), Taixi (K. 3) and
Hegu (L.I. 4). The pain was stopped after retaining needles for 5
minutes."

10. Trigeminal Neuralgia

Trigeminal nerves are divided into three branches: supra-
orbital branch, maxillary branch and mandibular branch. Trigeminal neuralgia occurs within the nerve innervation area accompanied by abrupt paroxysmal and temporary acute pain. It is a
kind of pricking or burning pain lasting for several seconds to
several minutes. Many attacks may occur in one day, often induced by washing the face, brushing the teeth or the intake of
food.

Treatment

Main points: Neiting (St. 44), Hegu (L.I. 4), Xiaguan (St. 7).

Method: Firstly puncture Neiting (St. 44), Hegu (L.I. 4) and

Xiaguan (St. 7), then combine other points according to different symptoms. Take the pain of the supra-orbital ridge (first branch), puncture Yangbai (G.B. 14) towards Yuyao (Extra) with a longer needle, or penetrate from Taiyang (Extra) to Shuaigu (G.B. 8); for the pain of maxillary branch spreading to the cheek, puncture Sibai (St. 2) towards Nose-Juliao (St. 3); for the pain of mandibular branch spreading to the lower gum, puncture Jiache (St. 6) towards Dicang (St. 4). Use the reducing method for the above points with its retention of needles for more than 30 minutes.

Typical case: Male, 23 years of age.

"He came to the hospital on June 3, 1985 after repeated occurrence of right facial pain for two months, and aggravation for two days. He complained that the first attack had accompanied the growth of a lower tooth on the right side. The intermittent pain had continued for half a year and remained even after the tooth-extraction. He was then diagnosed as trigeminal neuralgia and treated in a hospital by local blockage with anesthetics. There was a little improvement of his condition. The attacks persisted after Western medical treatment. Finally he went to see a dentist and had another tooth-extraction, there was no improvement. He again received local blockage treatment being injected of hydrochloride procaine, and the pain remained. Acupuncture treatment was suggested at this time. Neiting (St. 44), Hegu (L.I. 4), Taiyang (Extra) and Xiaguan (St. 7) were punctured with the reducing method, retaining the needles for 30 minutes. The pain was remarkably relieved. The patient was treated once every day, and cured after 10 days' treatment. Another 5 treatments were given despite the absence of pain, in order to verify the effectiveness."

11. Low Back Pain

Low back pain is a commonly seen symptom-complex in the clinic. Pain location is on one side, or both sides, or in the middle of the spine. Traditional Chinese medicine considers that "the waist is the house of the kidney," and the lower back is related to the kidney and connects with related channels. Thus low back pain has a close relationship with the kidney.

Differentiation

1. Cold-damp type

Low back pain usually occurs after exposure to pathogenic wind, cold and damp. For example, wear wet and cold dress after profuse sweating, sit or lie on damp ground, walk in the rain, etc. Therefore, pathogenic wind, cold and damp obstruct the channels blocking the circulation of Qi and blood. Clinical manifestations are heaviness, numbness and aching in the low back region, stiffness of muscles limiting extension and flexion of the back. The pain may radiate downward to the buttocks and lower extremities, and the affected area usually feels cold. Pain becomes intensified on cloudy and rainy days and is not alleviated by bed rest, there is white-sticky tongue coating and deep pulse.

2. Overstrain type

The patient has a history of sprain or trauma of the lumbar region causing Qi stagnation and blood stasis in the channels. When the lower back is overstrained, there is poor circulation of Qi and blood. Clinical manifestations are rigidity and pain of the lower back. The pain is fixed and aggravated by pressure strain, or turning of the body. There are no changes of the tongue and pulse.

3. Qi-Xu (deficiency) of the kidney type

This is due to kidney Qi-Deficiency in elderly people or after chronic disease. Stress and excessive sexual activities also exhaust kidney essence and blood, leaving the tendons and bones unnourished. Onset is subtle. Pain is mild but protracted. If it is complicated with lassitude, coldness and weakness of the lumbar region and knee, involuntary seminal discharge, thready pulse, these are the signs of kidney-Yang deficiency. While if it is accompanied by general weakness and irritability, yellow urine, rapid pulse and red tongue proper, these are symptoms of kidney-Yin deficiency.

140

Treatment

Method: To select the points on the channels of Taiyang, Shaoyang and Shaoyin of foot and Du Channel. The methods of reinforcing and reducing are given accordingly to different conditions of Xu or Shi. Or use the method of even movements of reinforcing and reducing. Acupuncture and moxibustion can be applied together.

Prescription: Shenshu (U.B. 23), Weizhong (U.B. 40), local points or Ashi points. Points added according to symptoms of cold-damp type: Fengfu (Du 16), Yaoyangguan (Du 3).

Overstrain type: Geshu (U.B. 17), Ciliao (U.B. 32).

Kidney Xu type: Mingmen (Du 4), Zhishi (U.B. 52), Taixi (K. 3). For severe onset of lumbago or acute lumbar sprain, reduce Renzhong (Du 26), or prick Weizhong (U.B. 40) with three-edged needle to cause bleeding, and then do cupping.

Remarks:

1. Low back pain may be seen in soft tissue injury, renal diseases, muscular rheumatism, rheumatoid diseases, or other pathological changes of internal organs.

2. Acupuncture treatment for various types of lumbago can get fairly good results. Puncturing local points is not suitable for the low back pain caused by spinal tuberculosis or tumor.

3. Empirical points and method: Puncture Huantiao (G.B. 30) and Weizhong (U.B. 40) of the affected side by standing erectly with the upper part of the body bending over by a desk or a bed. The erect legs form a 90-degree angle with the ground and separate as far as the width of the shoulder. Give strong stimulation without retaining the needle. Take the needle out as soon as the acupuncture sensation travels down to the foot. Ask the patient to stamp his feet 3-5 times. Then let the patient sit on a stool, and puncture Yanglingquan (G.B. 34) without retention of the needle. Finally ask the patient to walk erectly, twist the waist bilaterally, and do the movement of extension and flexion of the legs. Generally an immediate result can be obtained soon after acupuncture manipulation, and the patient who has had short term low back pain could be cured after 1-3 treatments.

For acute lumbar sprain Renzhong (Du 26), Yanglao (S.I. 6), Zanzhu (U.B. 2) are used as empirical points and can get unexpected immediate effectiveness. Ask the patient to move lower back during the manipulation of needles.

12. Chest and Hypochondriac Pain

This kind of chest and hypochondriac pain is aggravated by the movements of respiration. Known as "Cha Qi" (blocking Qi) in Chinese, it mostly occurs on one side with pricking pain or electric shock sensation. It is exasperated by cough or deep breathing. Severe cases may have related pain to the shoulder and back of the affected side. It is mostly caused by costal chondritis, trauma, simple intercostal neuralgia, or pleuritis. Acupuncture treatment is very effective.

Treatment

Main points: Yanglao (S.I. 6), Zhigou (S.J. 6), Neiguan (P. 6), Gongsun (Sp. 4).

Combined points: Yanglingquan (G.B. 34), Xuanzhong (G.B. 39), Shanzhong (Ren 17).

Method: Yanglao (S.I. 6) can be first punctured on the affected side for the chest and hypochondriac pain caused by various factors. Insert the needle rapidly and give strong stimulation. Take the needle out after sensation. Then ask the patient to do deep breathing until pain is stopped. Or puncture Gongsun (Sp. 4) first instead of Yanglao (S.I. 6) with the reducing method of lifting and thrusting the needle, or insert the needle into Neiguan (P. 6) with reinforcing method of lifting and thrusting the needle. Retention of the needle for the above points. Generally pain can be stopped immediately after withdrawal of the needle. If there is not much improvement, Zhigou (S.J. 6) or Yanglingquan (G.B. 34) should be added with rapid insertion and strong stimulation without retenting the needles.

Typical case: Female, 50 years of age.

"On June 15, 1985 she came to our hospital because of left chest and hypochondriac pain. She complained that on June 14, she began to have the pain spreading to the back, aggravated by the movements of respiration. Acute and intolerable pain occurred with deep breathing. We punctured Yanglao (S.I. 6) of the affected side. Pain was relieved soon after she got the acupuncture sensation. She went away with a smile."

13. Shoulder Pain

Shoulder pain is named in Traditional Chinese medicine as "leaking shoulder wind," or "frozen shoulder" or "fifty (years old) shoulder." It is seen mostly among people of about fifty years old who have weakness and deficiency of Ying (nutrient) and Wei (defensive) Qi. The exogenous pathogenic wind, cold and dampness can overcome persons who are exhausted, overstrained, injured or even asleep, by attacking the body at the shoulder. Once lodged in the shoulder, these exogenous pathogenic factors obstruct the circulation of Qi and blood through the channels, disrupting related tendon and muscle functions. Clinical manifestations are soreness and aching of one or both shoulders at the acute stage, pain radiating up to the neck region or down to the whole arm, more severe at night than daytime. The affected side is over-sensitive to cold with numbness and distension of fingers, stiffness of shoulder joint and limited lateral rotation, extension, and raising up of the affected arm. For chronic cases there might be muscular atrophy due to obstruction of pathogenic cold damp in tendons and muscles. Shoulder pain is in the scope of Bi syndrome in traditional Chinese medicine. If it is wind-Bi, it would be mostly due to the injury of tendon, manifested by the pain in the nape, back and fingers. If it is cold-Bi, it would be due to an injury of the tendons accompanied by severe pain that is ameliorated by warmth and pressure. If it is damp-Bi, it means that muscles are injured with a fixed location of pain, and swelling and distension of the affected area which is not eased by pressure.

Treatment

Method: To disperse wind and cold, remove dampness and obstruction of channels by puncturing the points of three Yang channels of hand with the reducing method. Moxibustion is advisable but not for those who have a burning sensation in the affected side.

Prescription: Jianyu (L.I. 15), Jianzhen (S.I. 9), Binao (L.I. 14), Quchi (L.I. 11), Waiguan (S.J. 5).

Points added according to the symptoms:

Pain of the medial side of the shoulder: Chize (Lu. 5), Taiyuan (Lu. 9).

Pain at the lateral aspect of the shoulder: Houxi (S.I. 3), Xiaohai (S.I. 8).

Pain at the anterior aspect of the shoulder: Hegu (L.I. 4), Lieque (Lu. 7).

Other secondary points: Ashi points, Jianneiling (Extra), Quyuan (S.I. 13), Dashu (U.B. 11), Fengchi (G.B. 20), Shousanli (L.I.10), Jianliao (S.J. 14), Tianrong (S.I. 17).

Remarks:

1. Shoulder pain here corresponds to perifocal inflammation of the shoulder.

2. Empirical points and methods: Distal points to the shoulder region, like Tiaokou (St. 38) and Chengshan (U.B. 57), can be used together for penetration needling. Let the patient sit with the legs flexed forming a right angle. Use a 2-3 *cun* long needle inserting it slowly from Tiaokou (St. 38) to Chengshan (U.B. 57). Rotate the needle continuously. After the patient has the acupuncture sensation, ask him to raise his affected arm up, or to rotate it backward to touch the back, or to reach the opposite shoulder. All these movements should be done gently, with no force. Retain the needle for 30 minutes. This method is suitable for acute cases but not good for chronic or old and weak patients.

3. In the later stages of perifocal inflammation of the shoulder, when the joint stiffens, exercise of the shoulder must be used in combination with acupuncture.

14. Stiff Neck

Stiff neck is a common symptom caused by exogenous pathogenic wind and cold or an awkward sleeping posture. Pain and motor impairment of the neck region are the main clinical manifestations, usually discovered after getting up in the morning. Severe cases may have the pain spread to the shoulder of the affected side, with aggravation by movements of the neck. There is obvious local tenderness without redness and swelling.

Treatment

Main points: Xuanzhong (G.B. 39), Houxi (S.I. 3), Yanglao (S.I. 6), Yanglingquan (G.B. 34).

Combined points: Inner-Hegu (L.I. 4), Fengchi (G.B. 20), Ashi point, Dazhui (Du 14), Zhizheng (S.I. 7), Tianzhu (U.B. 10), Luozhen (Extra).

Method: First puncture one or two of the main points such as Xuanzhong (G.B. 39) and Houxi (S.I. 3) or Yanglao (S.I. 6) and Yanglingquan (G.B. 34) making the acupuncture sensation spread to the affected neck region in order to get a better effect or puncture Luozhen (Extra) of the affected side. At the same time, ask the patient to move the head. Take the needles out after the pain is obviously relieved. Then one or two points can be combined locally. Cupping on Jianwaishu (S.I. 14) may be added for patients with neck pain spreading to the shoulder and back. Puncture Kunlun (U.B. 60) for difficult forward flexion and backward extension of the neck. For inability in turning, left and right Zhizheng (S.I. 7) can be punctured. If there is not much improvement, local moxibustion would be advisable. Generally one treatment may cure the patient.

Typical case: Female, 30 years of age.

"One day in September 1968, a patient came to the clinic because of right neck pain spreading to the shoulder for half a day. She explained that her neck pain was due to improper sleeping posture one day before she came. The pain was accompanied by motor impairment of the neck and exasperated by movements. She was treated by puncturing Xuanzhong (G.B. 39) with an immediate acupuncture sensation flowing to the shoulder and neck regions. The needle was retained for 15 minutes while the patient was asked to move the head and neck. The pain was relieved as soon as the treatment was finished."

15. Tennis Elbow

This happens among people who work with rotation of forearm or extension and flexion of elbow joint, or among those who have a history of exposure to cold and wind. The main clinical manifestations are pain of the lateral side of the elbow, which is more painful during extension or rotation of the elbow. Acupuncture is very effective for this kind of pain.

Treatment

Main point: Ashi point.

Combined points: Quchi (L.I. 11), Zhouliao (L.I. 12), Yanglingquan (G.B. 34).

Method: First let the patient move his affected elbow joint in order to find out the most painful point and position. Or determine the correspondent point on the healthy side to the painful point of the affected side. Rapidly insert the needle into the painful Ashi point or the corresponding point of the healthy side and give strong stimulation. Withdraw the needle soon after the presence of needling sensation. Pain can be stopped immediately after acupuncture manipulation. If there is not much improvement, the same manipulating method can be repeated on Quchi (L.I. 11) and Yanglingquan (G.B. 34).

Typical case: Male, 35 years of age.

"He came to our clinic three days after he got acute soreness aching of right elbow joint. He complained that three days ago, he had sprain of his right elbow due to lifting up heavy things followed by the pain and motor impairment of the elbow joint. The pain was exacerbated by movements of the arm. Treatment was given on the Ashi point of the lateral side of the right elbow joint with rapid insertion of the needle and strong stimulation. Pain disappeared immediately after the needling without retention of the needle."

16. Heel Pain

This symptom is commonly seen in the clinic. The frequent causes of it are calcaneal spur, infracalcaneal bursitis, sprain or degeneration of the calcaneal region. The main clinical manifestations are severe heel pain creating soreness upon heel contact with the ground and difficulty in walking. It occurs on both sides but one of the two sides may be severer than the other with a disease duration of a few weeks, months or years.

Treatment

Main point: Xiaguan (St. 7).

Combined points: Taixi (K. 3), Ashi point

Method: Xiaguan (St. 7) is used for heel pain caused by various reasons, with strong stimulation and rapid insertion of the needle. Generally retain the needle for 20-30 minutes. Another method is to insert the needles surrounding the most painful area of the heel. Most of the patients can be cured after several treatments with the above methods.

Typical case 1: Male, 58 years of age.

"He came to the hospital on June 12, 1985, because he had bad heel pain for two months. Right side was severer than the left side and he had difficulty in walking, X-ray examination showed bursitis of the calcaneal region. Treatment was given by puncturing Xiaguan (St. 7). Let the patient walk freely during retention of the needle. The pain was remarkably relieved after a few minutes of needling. Pain was stopped after 30 minutes of retaining the needle. The patient was treated once a day. He was cured after several treatments."

Typical case 2: Female, 40 years of age.

"She came to our clinic after she had bad heel pain on both sides for one year, recently increasing in severity. She complained that the right heel pain was worse. It occurred especially after getting up in the morning or long-time sitting. She had difficulty resting her on the ground and walking was difficult. Treatment was given by puncturing Xiaguan (St. 7) of the right side with strong stimulation and retention of the needle for 30 minutes. Pain stopped soon after the acupuncture. The patient was cured after one treatment. Follow-up was done for one week showing conclusive results."

17. Vomiting

Vomiting is a common symptom in the clinic occurring together with other diseases. It is due to disharmony and upward reversal of stomach-Qi caused by pathogenic wind, cold, summer-humidness, phlegm-humor, food accumulation or liver-Qi disorders.

Differentiation

1. Cold type: It is due to pathogenic cold invading in the epigastric region manifested by vomiting with clear water or saliva after the intake of food, white tongue coating and retarded pulse, preference of warmth, fear for cold, or loose stool.

2. Heat type: It is due to pathogenic heat accumulating inside, manifested by vomiting caused by the over-intake of food, vomiting with sour and bitter content and with foul smell, thirst, preference for cold, aversion to warmth, constipation, rapid pulse and yellow tongue coating.

3. Phlegm-humor stagnation type: This is due to phlegm-humor obstruction in the spleen and stomach or, over-intake of raw, cold and oily food, or it may be due to liver-Qi transversely attacking the stomach and forcing stomach-Qi to flow downward. This could result from emotional disturbance. The symptoms are fullness of chest, dizziness and vertigo, vomiting with mucus, or palpitation, white tongue coating and slippery pulse, or hypochondriac pain, acid regurgitation and wiry pulse.

4. Retention of food type: It is due to an over-intake of food resulting in indigestion and manifested by epigastric and abdominal pain and distension, acid fermented vomitus, belching, constipation, foul gas, thick and sticky tongue coating, slippery and Shi pulse.

5. Weakness of stomach-Qi: Intermittent vomiting, lack of appetite, slightly loose stools, general lassitude, forceless pulse, thin and sticky tongue coating.

Treatment

Method: Select the points of Foot-Yangming Channel as the main points. Retain the needles and apply moxibustion for cold type of vomiting. Swiftly withdraw the needles without moxibustion for heat type. Reduce the points of Foot-Jueyin Channel and reinforce the points of Foot-Yangming Channel for liver-Qi attacking stomach type. Simultaneously reinforce spleen-Qi while treating weakness of stomach-Qi.

Prescription: Zhongwan (Ren 12), Neiguan (P. 6), Zusanli (St. 36), Gongsun (Sp. 4).

Secondary points:

Heat type: Hegu (L.I. 4), Jinjin (Extra), Yuye (Extra).

Cold type: Shangwan (Ren 13), Weishu (U.B. 21).

Phlegm-humor: Shanzhong (Ren 17), Fenglong (St. 40).

Retention of food: Xiawan (Ren 10), Xuanji (Ren 21).

Liver-Qi: Yanglingquan (G.B. 34), Taichong (Liv. 3).

Weakness of stomach and spleen: Pishu (U.B. 20), Zhangmen (Liv. 13).

Remarks:

1. Vomiting occurs in acute gastritis, hepatitis, spasm or obstruction of cardia and pylorus, pancreatitis, cholecystitis, etc.

2. The acupuncture treatment described above can be used for vomiting of morning sickmen and drug response.

3. For belching, moxibustion can be applied on the Jianshi (P. 5).

4. Acupuncture treatment is effective for vomiting. But other treatments for the primary disease that causes vomiting is very important, such as serious obstruction of the upper digestive system, tumor or cerebral disorders.

5. Case report: One patient suffered from gastrectasia accompanied by intermittent nausea and vomiting. The patient was admitted to the hospital, but the disease condition gradually worsened after various kinds of treatment, Then acupuncture treatment was applied by using Zusanli (St. 36), Hegu (L.I. 4) and Weishu (U.B. 21) bilaterally. The patient was initially treated twice a day, needles were retained for 5 minutes. In the morning of the first treatment, the patient soon felt better and vomiting stopped. In the afternoon the patient had one bowel movement with soft stool, and the abdominal distension was relieved. After

3 days of treatment, there was no more vomiting or abdominal distension. The patient recovered and was discharged from the hospital.

18. Hiccup

Hiccup is caused by spasm of the diaphragm muscle which may be induced by emotional disturbance or the intake of cold or raw food. The hiccup cannot be controlled by the patient and exists for a few minutes, a few hours or even a longer time affecting the diet.

Treatment

Main points: Neiguan (P. 6), Zhongwan (Ren 12), Yifeng (S.J. 17).

Combined points: Tiantu (Ren 22).

Method: Firstly puncture Neiguan (P. 6) and Zhongwan (Ren 12), or singly Yifeng (S.J. 17) with strong stimulation and rotating the needle for several minutes. Generally hiccup can be stopped after the above manipulation. If it is not yet stopped Tiantu (Ren 22) could be punctured with a 1-1.5 *cun* needle and strong stimulation by the manipulating method of rotating the needle without retention of the needle.

For a weak patient, Zusanli (St. 36) and Qihai (Ren 6) can be added. For a patient with stagnation of liver-Qi, Taichong (Liv. 3) can be used in addition.

19. Epigastric Pain

Epigastric pain is also known as "heart-orifice pain" in Chinese, i.e. stomachache. Upper abdominal pain is the main clinical manifestation. It is commonly seen in gastroduodenal ulcer, acute and chronic gastritis, gastric neurosis, etc. It may be induced by irregular diet, mental stress, emotional depression or other factors.

Treatment

Main points: Neiguan (P. 6), Zhongwan (Ren 12), Zusanli (St.

150

36), Gongsun (Sp. 4).

Combined points: Ganshu (U.B. 18), Weishu (U.B. 21), Pishu (U.B. 20), Taichong (Liv. 3), Yanglingquan (G.B. 34).

Method: During the attack, puncture Zhongwan (Ren 12) first with rapid insertion but without retention of needle. Withdraw the needle as soon as the acupuncture sensation appears. Then puncture Neiguan (P. 6), Gongsun (Sp. 4), Zusanli (St. 36), and retain the needles after getting the acupuncture sensation. Apply the manipulating method of lifting, thrusting and rotating the needle once every 10 minutes until the relief of the pain. Generally after 10-30 minutes' manipulation of needles the pain may be remarkably relieved or completely stopped. If there is no much improvement, Ganshu (U.B. 18) and Pishu (U.B. 20) can be added. If the pain spreads to the hypochondriac regions, Taichong (Liv. 3) and Yanglingquan (G.B. 34) should be combined. Moxibustion is advisable on Weishu (U.B. 21) and Pishu (U.B. 20) for pain caused by cold factor.

20. Abdominal Pain

Abdominal pain is a common clinical symptom. Many diseases may cause abdominal pain, such as diseases of the biliary, gastro-intestinal, urinary and gynecological tracts. It can be classified into upper abdominal pain, lower abdominal pain, pain around umbilicus and lower lateral abdominal pain.

Treatment

Main points: Hegu (L.I. 4), Taichong (Liv. 3), Zusanli (St. 36), Sanyinjiao (Sp. 6).

Method: First puncture the above points with strong stimulation. If there is not much improvement, the following points could be added accordingly:

Upper abdominal pain: Zhongwan (Ren 12), Liangmen (St. 21), or Ganshu (U.B. 18), Weishu (U.B. 21).

Lower abdominal pain: Guanyuan (Ren 4), Zhongji (Ren 3), or Shenshu (U.B. 23), Dachangshu (U.B. 25).

Pain around umbilicus: Tianshu (St. 25), Qihai (Ren 6).

Lower lateral abdominal pain: Yanglingquan (G.B. 34), Zhangmen (Liv. 13), Jingmen (G.B. 25).

Pain complicated with vomiting: Neiguan (P. 6).

Pain with fever: Dazhui (Du 14), Quchi (L.I. 11).

Biliary ascariases: Puncture from Yingxiang (L.I. 20) towards Sibai (St. 2), Dannang (Extra, tender spot 1-2 *cun* below Yanglingquan, G.B. 34).

Pain of appendicitis: Lanwei (Extra, tender spot 1.5 *cun* below Zusanli, St. 36).

21. Diarrhea

Diarrhea indicates frequent movement of bowels with loose or watery stools. Acute diarrhea is mostly due to contaminated food or injury of the stomach and intestines caused by an over-intake of food and drink. It is manifested by abrupt abdominal pain, borborygmus, diarrhea, or even with fever. Chronic diarrhea is often caused by Yang-Xu (deficiency) of spleen and kidney and manifested by dull abdominal pain, loose stools 2-3 times a day, anorexia, lassitude, etc. Most of the symptoms belong to the scope of acute and chronic enteritis, intestinal tuberculosis, etc.

Treatment

Main points: Tianshu (St. 25), Shenque (Ren 8), Zusanli (St. 36).

Combined points: Hegu (L.I. 4), Quchi (L.I. 11), Zhongwan (Ren 12), Neiguan (P. 6), Guanyuan (Ren 4), Yinlingquan (Sp. 9), Pishu (U.B. 20), Shenshu (U.B. 23).

Method: Firstly puncture Tianshu (St. 25), Zusanli (St. 36) and do moxibustion on the Shenque (Ren 8) point. Then add some points according to the other symptoms.

Fever with aversion to cold: Quchi (L.I. 11), Hegu (L.I. 4).

Vomiting: Zhongwan (Ren 12), Neiguan (P. 6).

Dehydration: Moxibustion on Guanyuan (Ren 4).

Acute cases: Puncture Quchi (L.I. 11), prick Weizhong (U.B. 40) with three-edged needle to let the blood out.

Chronic cases: Pishu (U.B. 20), Weishu (U.B. 21), Shenshu

(U.B. 23), Mingmen (Du 4), Qihai (Ren 6), and plus moxibustion after needling.

22. Dysentery

This condition is an infectious intestinal disease which mostly occurs in summer and autumn mainly manifested by abdominal pain, tenesmus, dysentery with blood and pus. It is divided into damp-heat, cold-damp, chronic type and vomiting types.

1. Damp-heat type: It is mostly due to exogenous pathogenic factors and food accumulation and obstruction in the intestines caused by an invasion of summer-humidness and the intake of contaminated food or cold and raw food. Thus the large intestine loses its function of transportation that pathogenic damp and heat struggle against each other leading to stagnation of Qi and blood and injuring the vessels and Zang-Fu organs. It results in dysentery with blood and pus. If pathogenic heat is preponderant, it will damage the blood being manifested by more blood and less pus in the stools. If pathogenic damp is excessive, it will injure the Qi and be manifested by more pus and less blood. Main symptoms are abdominal pain, dysentery with blood and pus, tenesmus accompanied by burning sensation of anus, scanty and yellow urine, slippery and rapid pulse, and yellow- sticky tongue coating, or even chill and fever, irritability and thirst.

2. Cold-damp type: It is due to constitutional weakness of stomach and spleen, especially Qi weakness of these two organs. The pathogenic wind-cold or summer-humidness attacks the body when it is weak. The pathogenic cold and damp stagnate inside the body. The resulting manifestations are: diarrhea with sticky and white mucus, preference of warmth and dislike of coldness, fullness of chest and sticky tongue coating, soft, slow or tardy pules.

3. Chronic type: Also known as the "rest dysentery" in traditional Chinese medicine with repeated occurrences for a long time, intermittent mildness or severeness, dysentery with pus and blood, abdominal pain, tenesmus, suspended dry or loose stools.

4. Vomiting type: Dysentery with blood and pus, character-ized by serious vomiting causing difficult in food intake.

Treatment

Method: To regulate the Qi circulation in the large intestine in order to clear up damp-heat or cold-damp by puncturing the points of the Foot-Yangming channel as the main points together with the points of the kidney, spleen and urinary bladder chan-nels. Moxibustion is advisable for the cold type.

Prescription: Hegu (L.I. 4), Tianshu (St. 25).

Dámp-heat type: Quchi (L.I. 11), Neiting (St. 44), Shangjuxu (St. 37).

Cold-damp type: Zhongwan (Ren 12), Qihai (Ren 6).

Chronic type: Pishu (U.B. 20), Weishu (U.B. 21), Guanyuan (Ren 4), Shenshu (U.B. 23).

Vomiting type: Zhongwan (Ren 12), Neiting (St. 44).

Tenesmus: Zhonglushu (U.B. 29).

Anus prolapse: Moxibustion on Baihui (Du 20).

Remarks:

1. Acupuncture treatment has a satisfactory result for dysen-tery. But in dangerous and acute stage of bacillary dysentery, the comprehensive treatment and emergency measures should be applied.

2. During the onset of dysentery, strict regulation of diet and adequate sanitation are necessary, including consumption of clean or boiled water and light food, while avoiding uncooked food.

3. It was reported that in 645 cases with positive cultures, the changes in clinical manifestations and stool cultures from posi-tive to negative were observed. All the cases had abdominal pain, red and white mucus in stools, tenesmus, etc. Points Qihai (Ren 6), Tianshu (St. 25) (both sides) and Shangjuxu (St. 37) (both sides) were added. The reducing method of manipulation was used. Needles were retained for 30-60 minutes. Treatment was given 1-3 times a day according to the severity of the disease. Ten times of treatment were taken as one course. The therapeutic result was that 596 cases were cured in one course of treatment (92.4 percent).

23. Constipation

Constipation is a condition in which the bowel movements are infrequent or incomplete, the consistency being dry and hard, and the feces being retained in the intestines for more than two days. This disease can be divided into Shi or Xu types.

Differentiation

1. Shi type: It is mostly due to body constitutional Yang-excess and over-indulgence of pungent, hot or fatty food causing the accumulation of heat in the stomach and intestines; or it is due to pathogenic heat consuming the body fluid causing the obstruction and dryness of intestines; or it is due to overflow of emotions disturbing the Qi functions which fail to spread body fluid throughout the body. Thus the intestine loses its function of conduction resulting in constipation. The symptoms are a decrease in the number of bowel movements, usually once every three or five days or more. They are dry and hard. If there is excessive pathogenic heat, it would be manifested by fever, irritability, thirst, foul smell in mouth, preference of cold food and drinks, slippery and Shi pulse, yellow and dry tongue coating. In severer condition of Qi-stagnation, there would be fullness and pain of hypochondriac and abdominal regions, frequent belching, poor appetite, wiry pulse and thin-sticky tongue coating.

2. Xu type: This is mostly due to poor recovery of Qi and blood after a chronic disease or after delivery; or it is due to old age and weak body so that there is a great exhaustion of Qi and blood; that is, Qi-deficiency causes weakness of transportation and transformation, blood-deficiency makes the intestines lose the nourishment and moistness from the blood. Or it is due to Yang-Qi Xu (deficiency) of lower Jiao that Yin-cold is accumulated in intestines resulting in constipation. If it is caused by weakness and deficiency of Qi and blood, the symptoms would be pale and lusterless color of face, lips and nails, dizziness,

vertigo, palpitation, lassitude, shortness of breath, pale tongue proper with thin coating, weak and thready pulse. If it is caused by Yin-cold accumulation, the manifestations are coldness and pain in abdomen, preference of warmth or hot while dislike cold, deep and slow pulse, pale tongue proper with white and moist coating.

Treatment

Method: To regulate the function of transportation of intestines, to clear up the heat or cold from intestines and to adjust the Qi circulation of Sanjiao in order to remove the obstruction from intestines by puncturing the points of the large intestine channel, Sanjiao channel and Ren and stomach channels; and the back-Shu points of the urinary bladder channel. The reducing method is used for Shi type, while reinforcing method is used for Xu type. Moxibustion is applied to constipation together with cold symptoms.

Prescription: Dachangshu (U.B. 25), Tianshu (St. 25), Zhigou (S.J. 6), Shangjuxu (St. 37).

Heat accumulation: Hegu (L.I. 4), Quchi (L.I. 11).

Qi stagnation: Zhongwan (Ren 12), Xingjian (Liv. 2).

Deficiency of Qi and blood: Pishu (U.B. 20), Weishu (U.B. 21).

Cold constipation: Moxibustion on Shenque (Ren 8) and Qihai (Ren 6).

Remarks:

1. The habit of a bowel movement, at the same time every day, should be cultivated. Diet is very important. More vegetables and fruits are recommended.

2. Empirical points: Zhigou (S.J. 6) and Yanglingquan (G.B. 34) work in a pair for Shi type of constipation, while Sanyinjiao (Sp. 6) and Zhaohai (K. 6) are used for Xu type of constipation.

24. Prolapse of Anus

It is also called protrusion of the rectum with discharges of mucus which is sometimes found in children, elderly people and multiparous women.

Differentiation

This condition in traditional Chinese medicine is attributed to a weak physical constitution, prolonged diarrhea, dysentery and constipation, or giving birth too often. All of these factors may contribute to a weakening of constringency of the rectum which is caused by Qi of the middle Jiao sinking downward. It is manifested by gradual onset. At first a ring of bright red mucous membrane protrudes, as a result of straining at stool, which can reduce by itself. When the condition does not yield to simple treatment, it can be aroused by any straining and the protruded part must be restored by steady pressure with hands; or it is accompanied by lassitude, weakness of extremities, yellowish complexion, dizziness, vertigo, palpitation, soft and thready pulse, pale tongue proper with white coating. It can be differentiated into Shi or Xu type. Shi type is due to straining during bowel movement because of dry and hard stools accompanied by itching, redness, swelling or pricking pain. Xu type is caused by the sinking of Qi and manifested by general weakness, low spirit, or other weak symptoms.

Treatment

Method: To clear up the heat for Shi type, to reinforce Qi and to elevate Yang from prostration by puncturing the points mainly from the Du and Ren channels.

Shi type: Tianshu (St. 25), Dachangshu (U.B. 25), Zusanli (St. 36), Neiguan (P. 6).

Xu type: Moxibustion on Baihui (Du 20), Shenque (Ren 8) and Qihai (Ren 6), or puncture Changqiang (Du 1).

Remarks: Prolapse of rectum of constitutionally weak patients can be remedied by traditional medicinal herbs or oral administration of Western drugs.

25. Seminal Emission

Seminal emission may be involuntary or with dreams (nocturnal emission). Generally unmarried men may have spermatorrhea once a week; this is considered as a normal physiological phenomenon, it is not a pathological change.

Differentiation

1. Involuntary emission: The involuntary emission is usually due to chronic illness or excessive sexual activities or frequent masturbation, causing exhaustion of kidney essence. Loss of Yin may affect Yang. If it is Yin-deficiency (Xu), there would arouse of Xu-fire disturbing the "sperm house"; if it is Yang-deficiency (Xu), then the kidney would lose its function of storing essence leading to uncontrolled emission. The main symptoms are frequent seminal emission without dreams, soreness and coldness of low back, pale and lusterless complexion, lassitude, or sometimes accompanied by impotence, spontaneous sweating, shortness of breath, pale tongue proper with white coating, thready or thready-rapid pulse.

2. Nocturnal emission: It is mainly due to mental stress, anxiety or over-indulgence which leads to preponderance of heart-fire and exhaustion of kidney essence. Heart and pericardium fire can disturb the "spermatic house." An over-indulgence of fatty, sweet and spicy food causes the accumulation of damp and heat which pours downward to harass the spermatic house resulting in nocturnal emission. Main symptoms: Frequent emission during sleep with sexual dreams accompanied by pre-ejaculation, dizziness, insomnia, irritability, soreness and aching of the low back, ringing in the ears, yellow urine, red tongue proper, thready and rapid pulse.

Treatment

1. Nocturnal emission with dreams:

Method: To clear up the heart-fire to nourish Yin and recapture the essence by puncturing the points of the channels of urinary bladder, Ren and Foot-Jueyin, with the reducing method.

Prescription: Xinshu (U.B. 15), Shenshu (U.B. 23), Guanyuan (Ren 4), Zhongfeng (Liv. 4).

Insomnia: Shenmen (H. 7), Neiguan (P. 6), Lidui (St. 45).

Dizziness: Baihui (Du 20).

2. Involuntary emission:

Method: To reinforce kidney-Qi and consolidate the essence by puncturing the points of Ren, urinary bladder and Foot-Taiyin channels with the reinforcing method or moxibustion.

Prescription: Shenshu (U.B. 23), Qihai (Ren 6), Sanyinjiao (Sp. 6), Zhishi (U.B. 52).

Spontaneous sweating: Yinxi (H. 6), Zusanli (St. 36).

Shortness of breath: Feishu (U.B. 13).

Remarks:

1. During acupuncture treatment, the doctor should help the patient overcome psychological anxiety and those factors which cause seminal emission; instruct the patient with knowledge of mental hygiene and to establish a good habits; guide the patient to do exercises in order to enhance the effectiveness of acupuncture.

2. The acupuncture sensation of Guanyuan (Ren 4) or Zhongji (Ren 3) should propagate to balance, and the sensation of San-yinjiao (Sp. 6) should flow to the sole or medial aspect of the knee.

26. Impotence

Impotence is generally due to damage of kidney-Yang resulting from repeated seminal emission or excessive sexual activities. It may also be due to damaged heart, spleen and kidney-Qi resulting from emotional factors such as fright and worry. It can be divided into Xu and Shi types.

Differentiation

1. Xu type: It is characterized by inability of penile erection, repeated emission, with thin and clear sperm. In case of insufficiency of kidney-Yang, there may appear pallor, dizziness, ring in the ears, low spirit, pale tongue proper, thready and weak pulse. If it is accompanied by the injury of heart-Qi and spleen-Qi, palpitation and insomnia may be present.

2. Shi type: This is characterized by a short period of penile erection complicated with pre-ejaculation, wet and foul smell of the scrotum, heaviness and soreness of lower limbs, yellow urine, yellow and sticky tongue coating, soft and rapid pulse.

Treatment

Method: Apply acupuncture with the reinforcing method plus moxibustion to points of the Ren and kidney channels to tonify the kidney-Yang and at the same time to clear up the damp heat.

Prescription: Shenshu (U.B. 23), Guanyuan (Ren 4), Yinlingquan (Sp. 9), Zusanli (St. 36), Mingmen (Du 4), Taixi (K. 3), Rangu (K. 2), Baliao (U.B. 31, 32, 33, 34).

27. Dizziness and Vertigo

This condition indicates that the patient feels giddy and dizzy accompanied by nausea, vomiting, perspiration, etc. It can be seen in hypertension, arteriosclerosis, internal auditory vertigo, anemia, neurasthenia, etc. It is divided into Xu and Shi types.

Differentiation

1. Xu type: It is due to Xu (deficiency) of the heart and spleen and insufficient formation of Qi and blood caused by weak body constitution and mental overstrain. Or it is due to insufficiency of the "sea of marrow" in the head caused by excessive sexual activities leading to exhaustion of kidney-Yin that fails to fill up the brain marrow. Main symptoms are giddiness and blurred vision, aggravation or recurrence due to overstraining, lusterless complexion, lassitude, palpitation, insomnia, soreness and low back-chain, ringing in the ears, pale tongue proper and thready pulse.

2. Shi type: It is due to liver-Yang preponderance and liver-wind stirring caused by emotional anger that affects the liver; or it is due to excessive damp changing into pathogenic phlegm which disturbs the head together with liver-Yang and liver-wind caused by body constitution, fatty or over-indulgence of sweet and fatty food. Clinical manifestations are: intermittent dizziness and vertigo characterized by spinning sensation, pain and distension of the head, heaviness of the head like "cloth wrapped around the head," irritability, fullness and distension of the chest and hypochondriac regions, nausea, vomiting with saliva, poor appetite, red tongue proper with thick-sticky or floating yellow

coating, wiry or slippery-rapid pulse.

Treatment

1. Xu type

Method: To reinforce and cultivate Qi and blood by selecting the points on the urinary bladder, Du, Foot-Shaoyang or Yangming channels with the reinforcing method of acupuncture or with moxibustion.

Prescription: Baihui (Du 20), Fengchi (G.B. 20), Geshu (U.B. 17), Zusanli (St. 36).

Palpitation: Neiguan (P. 6).

Insomnia: Shenmen (H. 7).

Ringing in the ears: Tinggong (S.I. 19).

2. Shi type

Method: To pacify liver-Yang, harmonize the stomach and dissolve phlegm by selecting the points on the Ren and Du channels and three Yin channels of the foot with the reducing method of acupuncture and no moxibustion.

Prescription: Zhongwan (Ren 12), Yinlingquan (Sp. 9), Xingjian (Liv. 2), Shuiquan (K. 5), Yintang (Extra).

Hypochondriac distension: Yanglingquan (G.B. 34).

Heaviness of head: Touwei (St. 8).

Remarks:

1. The dizziness and vertigo caused by internal medical diseases mostly have no spinning sensation. Differentiation of it can be done from the primary diseases such as anemia, hypertension, neurasthenia, etc.

2. The internal auditory vertigo is characterized by intermittent onset with serious spinning sensation or feelings of shakiness, aggravated by the changing of posture and accompanied by ringing in the ears, deafness, nystagmus, etc.

3. If dizziness and vertigo are due to drug poisoning such as streptomycin, neomycin, kanamycin, etc., including serious damage of auditory nerve, acupuncture will be effective.

28. Deafness and Tinnitus

Deafness and ringing in the ears are manifestations of functional impairment of hearing. Many factors may cause these symptoms. Deafness shows the degeneration of hearing. While ringing in the ears means that the patient feels sounds in the ear, like cicadas, drum, bell, wind blowing, water flowing, etc. Traditional Chinese medicine divides it into Xu (deficiency) and Shi (excess) type. Xu type is caused by insufficiency of kidney essence and Qi manifested by intermittent ear ringing and cicada-like sounds while pressing the ear with hand. It is exasperated by overstrain and accompanied by weakness and soreness of the lower back and knees, thready and forceless pulse. The Shi type is mostly caused by the fire of liver and gall bladder, manifested by the sounds of drum or wind blowing. Pressing the hand on the ear will not relieve the ringing of ears. It is accompanied by dizziness, distension of the head, headache, wiry and forceful pulse.

Treatment

Main points; Tinggong (S.I. 19) or Tinghui (G.B. 2), Ermen (S.J. 21), Yifeng (S.J. 17), Hand-Zhongzhu (S.J. 3).

Combined points: Fengchi (G.B. 20), Hegu (L.I. 4), Xingjian (Liv. 2), Shenshu (U.B. 23), Taixi (K. 3), Waiguan (S.J. 5).

Method: Generally puncture Tinggong (S.I. 19), Yifeng (S.J. 17) and Hand-Zhongzhu (S.J. 3) first. If there shows little improvement, then Tinghui (G.B. 2), Waiguan (S.J. 5) and Hegu (L.I. 4) can be added. Patients of the Shi type can be punctured by selecting Fengchi (G.B. 20) and Xingjian (Liv. 2), while patients of Xu type can be treated by puncturing Shenshu (U.B. 23) and Taixi (K. 3).

29. Insomnia

Insomnia is a condition of sleeplessness. It can be intermittent or constant. It is accompanied by headache, dizziness, poor memory, lassitude, low spirit, etc. Actually these are the commonly seen symptoms in neurasthenia. Traditional Chinese medicine considers that it is due to deficiency of heart-Yin and spleen Qi, or incoordination between heart and kidney caused by overstrain leading to internal injury.

Treatment

Main points: Shenmen (H. 7), Neiguan (P. 6), Sanyinjiao (Sp. 6).

Combined points: Baihui (Du 20), Fengchi (G.B. 20), Taiyang (Extra), Zusanli (St. 36).

Method: Puncture Shenmen (H. 7), Neiguan (P. 6) and Sanyin-jiao (Sp. 6) with moderate or mild stimulation. Patients with less improvement after puncturing the above points can be treated by adding Anmian (Extra), midway between Fengchi (G.B. 20) and Yifeng (S.J. 17).

Dizziness: Fengchi (G.B. 20), Taiyang (Extra) and Baihui (Du 20).

Palpitation and poor memory: Ximen (P. 4).

Spermatorrhea and impotence: Guanyuan (Ren 4), Shenshu (U.B. 23).

Anorexia: Zusanli (St. 36), Zhongwan (Ren 12).

30. Palpitation

Palpitation is a common condition in which the heart beats forcibly or irregularly, and the patient feels weakness. It is often seen in arrhythmia caused by various reasons or cardial neurosis.

Treatment

Main points: Tianzhu (U.B. 10), Ximen (P. 4), Neiguan (P. 6), Shanzhong (Ren 17).

Combined points: Zusanli (St. 36), Fengchi (G.B. 20), Shenmen (H. 7), Jianshi (P. 5).

Method: Puncture Tianzhu (U.B. 10) first without retention of the needle. Then puncture Ximen (P. 4) by rotating the needle for 2-5 minutes. Palpitation may be relieved soon after manipulation. Or puncture Neiguan (P. 6) and Shanzhong (Ren 17) with the manipulation of vibrating the needle handle. If there is not much improvement, Sanyinjiao (Sp. 6) and Jianshi (P. 5) could be punctured with the manipulating method of lifting and thrusting the needle. Other points can be supplemented.

Dizziness: Fengchi (G.B. 20).
Weakness of four extremities: Zusanli (St. 36).
Bradycardia: Suliao (Du 25).
Tachycardia: Jianshi (P. 5).

31. Angina Pectoris

Angina pectoris is a term applied to a violent paroxysm of painful sensations in the chest, arising for the most part in connection with disease of the coronary arteries, such as arteriosclerosis, insufficient supply of heart blood of arteries, etc. A feature of angina pectoris is the occurrence of pain behind the sternum, or in the pericardium. The paroxysm of pain lasts a short time, usually 1-2 minutes, seldom longer than 15 minutes. It arises as a result of exertion and is relieved by rest.

Treatment

Main point: Neiguan (P. 6), Xinping (Extra), 3 *cun* below Shaohai (H. 3), Xinshu (U.B. 15), Jueyinshu (U.B. 14), Shanzhong (Ren 17), Juque (Ren 14).

Combined points: Jianshi (P. 5), Zusanli (St. 36), Guanyuan (Ren 4), Qihai (Ren 6), Sanyinjiao (Sp. 6).

Method: During the attack of angina pectoris, puncture Neiguan (P. 6) or Xinping (Extra) first with even movements of reinforcing and reducing. Acupuncture sensations of soreness, distension, tingling or numbness are required. If there is not much improvement, other points can be added, such as Zusanli (St. 36) and Jianshi (P. 5). For pale complexion and cold extremities do moxibustion on Guanyuan (Ren 4) and Qihai (Ren 6).

32. Hypertension

The basis for a diagnosis of hypertension among the people younger than 40 years old is usually taken to be a systolic pressure which is persistently greater than 140 mm Hg and a diastolic pressure which is persistently greater than 90 mm Hg. The systolic pressure would be increased 10 mm Hg for each ten additional years among people over 40 years old.

Aging usually does not cause an increase in diastolic pressure. Hypertension is often accompanied by symptoms of headache, dizziness, distension of head, ringing in the ears, insomnia, irritability, palpitation, etc. Hypertension can be divided into primary and secondary types. Primary hypertension is mostly caused by disorders of the higher level nerve system. Secondary hypertension is often aroused by nephritis, toxemia of pregnancy, and endocrine disorders of intracranial diseases.

Treatment

Main points: Quchi (L.I. 11), Fengchi (G.B. 20), Tianzhu (U.B. 10).

Combined points: Zusanli (St. 36), Taichong (Liv. 3), Hegu (L.I. 4), Taiyang (Extra).

Method: Puncture from Quchi (L.I. 11) towards Shaohai (H. 3), deep insertion is done in Tianzhu (U.B. 10) for 1-1.5 *cun*. There is no retention of needles. Or singly puncture Quchi (L.I. 11) with the reducing method of lifting, thrusting and rotating the needle. Blood pressure may be lower 30 minutes after acupuncture.

Headache, dizziness and distension of head: Taiyang (Extra), Fengchi (G.B. 20), Yintang (Extra), Hegu (L.I. 4), Taichong (Liv. 3).

Tinnitus: Waiguan (S.J. 5), Yifeng (S.J. 17).

Insomnia: Shenmen (H. 7), Sanyinjiao (Sp. 6).

Palpitation: Neiguan (P. 6), Ximen (P. 4).

Anorexia: Zusanli (St. 36).

Excessive phlegm: Fenglong (St. 40), Zhongwan (Ren 12).

33. Facial Paralysis

This has the common name "deviated mouth and eyes" and can occur at any age, but mostly among young and middle aged people. It is a simple flaccidity of one side of the face with acute onset but without hemiplegia or unconsciousness.

Differentiation

This disease is due to the weakness and deficiency of the channels and collateral which are easily attacked by the exogenous pathogenic wind-cold or wind-heat leading to the flaccidness of facial muscles because of Qi-stagnation and blood stasis of the musculotendinous channels of the facial region. It is manifested by sudden onset after sleep with dull complexion, numbness and paralysis of face, difficult sniffling, inability of frowning, showing teeth and blowing cheeks, mouth deviated towards the healthy side with salivation, food staying in between the teeth and cheek of the affected side, disappearance of forehead creases and of nasolabial groove, incomplete opening or closing of eyes, lacrimation due to exposure to wind. Some of the patients may have pain behind the ear or of the face. In severe çases, there may be disappearance or hypoactivity of a sense of taste over two-thirds of the tongue or hyperactivity of hearing. In the case of the wing-cold type, it is due to wind exposure during sleep or blowing by electric fan. There is no Exterior (Biao) symptom-complex. If it is wind-heat type, there would be secondary symptoms like fever, otitis media, pain and swelling of gums accompanied by slight pain of the inner ear or of mastoid process.

Treatment

Method: To select the points mainly from the Foot-Yangming channel, by acupuncture or needle penetration with the reducing method at the acute stage and the reinforcing method at the latter stage. Moxibustion is advisable.

Prescription: Dicang (St. 4), Jiache (St. 6), Taichong (Liv. 3), Taiyang (Extra), Hegu (L.I. 4), Yangbai (G.B. 14), Sibai (St. 2), Quanliao (S.I. 18), Xiaguan (St. 7).

Inability to sniffle: Zanzhu (U.B. 2).

Disappearance of the nasolabial groove: Yingxiang (L.I. 20).

Pain of the mastoid process: Yifeng (S.J. 17), Head-Wangu (G.B. 12).

Deviation of the mandibular labial groove: Chengjiang (Ren 24).

Numbness of the tongue and loss of sense of taste: Lianquan (Ren 23).

Incomplete closing of the eye: Jingming (U.B. 1), Tongziliao

(G.B. 1), Yuyao (Extra), Sizhukong (S.J. 23).

Remarks:

1. Acupuncture treatment should be combined with hot-wet compresses twice a day, ten minutes each time. Wind exposure should be avoided. Eye-drops can be used 2-3 times a day for foreign substances in the eye due to incomplete closing of the eye.

2. Data abstract: The observation of EMG changes during the acupuncture treatment of peripheral facial paralysis was done by a hospital. EMG before treatment showed most of the patients had complete or partial loss of facial nerve innervation and decreased excitation. After treatment most of the patients had the symptoms and signs relieved, nerve innervation regained and nerve functions recovered. Observation of immediate changes of the EMG of some patients showed that there was an obvious increase of electric potential frequency and peak value voltage of voluntary muscles among most of the patients who were treated by ear acupuncture. It indicates that acupuncture has immediate and benign regulatory action so as to enhance excitation of nerves, to improve local metabolism of nourishment and to speed up the recovery of muscle and nerve function.

34. Bi Symptom-Complex (Appendix: Sciatica)

"Bi" means obstruction or blockage. Those symptoms of pain, swelling, heaviness, distension or numbness or even the motor impairment of limbs caused by the invasion of exogenous patho- ogenic factors into the channels, muscles, joints leading to the blocking of the circulation of Qi and blood are named as Bi symptom-complex. It includes rheumatic fever, rheumatic arthritis, muscular fibrositis, sciatica, etc. It is classified as wandering Bi, painful Bi, fixed Bi and heat Bi because of different causative factors. And it also can be divided into skin Bi, muscular Bi, tendon Bi and bony Bi according to the depth of disease transmission. The deeper the disease location is, the severer the disease condition would be.

Differentiation

Wandering Bi: It tends to have exogenous pathogenic wind as the main causative factor manifested by mobile pain from joint to joint, unfixed pain, or pain of one place radiating distally with referred numbness just like rapid moving wind, difficult extension and flexion, or even chill and fever, thin and white tongue coating or slight yellow coating, superficial and wiry pulse.

Painful Bi: It has the exogenous pathogenic cold as the main factor of this condition manifested by acute pain of muscles and joints together with cold sensation, pain relieved by warmth and pressing while aggravated by cold, white and thin tongue coating, superficial and tense pulse.

Fixed Bi: Pathogenic damp is the main factor of this condition characterized by sore aching and heaviness of joints and body, slight swelling without redness, exacerbated by rainy, windy or cold weather, white sticky tongue coating, soft and weak pulse.

Heat Bi: The syndrome is due to wind-damp changing into heat manifested by sore aching of joints of the four limbs, with swelling and motor impairment accompanied by sore throat, fever with excessive sweating, scanty and yellowish urine, thick sticky and yellow tongue coating, soft and rapid pulse.

Treatment

Method: To disperse wind and cold, clear up heat and to dissolve damp in order to remove the obstruction of the musculotendinous channel, and to regulate the circulation of Qi and blood by selecting local points and the points of involved channels. Shallow puncturing or tapping with plum-blossom needle for the diseases located in skin and muscle, deep insertion and longer retention of needles for the diseases in tendons and bones; blood-letting method for diseases in the vessels.

Prescription:

Shoulder region: Jianliao (S.J. 14), Jianyu (L.I. 15), Naoshu (S.I. 10).

Elbow and forearm: Quchi (L.I. 11), Hegu (L.I. 4), Tianjing (S.J. 10), Waiguan (S.J. 5), Chize (Lu. 5).

Wrist region: Yangchi (S.J. 4), Waiguan (S.J. 5), Yangxi (L.I. 5),

Hand-Wangu (S.I. 4).

Back region: Renzhong (Du 26), Shenzhu (Du 12), Yaoyangguan (Du 3).

Hip region: Huantiao (G.B. 30), Femur-Juliao (G.B. 29), Xuanzhong (G.B. 39).

Femur region: Zhibian (U.B. 54), Chengfu (U.B. 36), Yinlingquan (Sp. 9).

Knee region: Dubi (St. 35), Liangqiu (St. 34), Yanglingquan (G.B. 34), Xiyangguan (G.B. 33).

Ankle region: Shenmai (U.B. 62), Zhaohai (K. 6), Kunlun (U.B. 60), Qiuxu (G.B. 40).

Points added accordingly:

Wandering Bi: Fengmen (U.B. 12), Geshu (U.B. 17), Ganshu (U.B. 18)

Painful Bi: Shenshu (U.B. 23), Guanyuan (Ren 4)

Fixed Bi: Pishu (U.B. 20), Zusanli (St. 36), Yinlingquan (Sp. 9)

Heat Bi: Dazhui (Du 14), Quchi (L.I. 11)

Remarks: Acupuncture treatment for 1,168 cases with Bi symptom-complex: 600 cases were cured, occupying 51.36 percent; 338 cases had remarkable effect (28.93 percent); 185 cases had improvement (15.83 percent); 45 cases had no result (3.85 percent). The total effective rate was 96.12 percent.

Appendix: Sciatica

Sciatica belongs to the scope of Bi symptom-complex characterized by radiating pain along part or the whole course of the pathway of sciatic nerve.

Differentiation

It is due to blockage by exogenous pathogenic wing-cold or damp-heat in the channels or it is due to the obstruction of Qi and blood in the channels caused by injuries from falls, fractures, contusions and strains. Since there is obstruction of channels there would be accompanying pain. If the illness is prolonged, and the tendons and muscles lose the nourishment from Qi and blood, there would be atrophy, numbness, cold pain or burning sensation of the gluteal muscles and the thigh and lower leg muscles. It is manifested by intermittent or constant leg pain characterized by burning pain and pricking pain in the hip region, along the posterior aspect of the thigh and lateral aspect of lower leg, down to the foot.

Pain is aggravated by movements. There are tender spots near Dachangshu (U.B. 25), Guanyuanshu (U.B. 26), Femur-Juliao (G.B. 29), Huantiao (G.B. 30), Heyang (U.B. 55), Chengshan (U.B. 57), Kunlun (U.B. 60), Yongquan (K. 1) causing difficulty to raise the leg. If it is caused by exogenous pathogenic wind-heat, the symptoms would be characterized by burning sensation in the limb which is exasperated by heat. If it is due to exogenous pathogenic wind-cold, the symptom would be characterized by a cold pain of the limb which is ameliorated by receiving warmth. If it is mixed with dampness, there would be heaviness and pain in the limb which is exacerbated by overcast and rainy weather.

Treatment

Method: To activate blood circulation, relax muscles and tendons and to stop pain by puncturing the points of the Foot-Taiyang and Foot-Shaoyang channels, or the points of the Foot-Yangming and Foot-Taiyin channels for muscular atrophy, with the reducing method. Moxibustion and cupping are advisable.

Prescription: Dachangshu (U.B. 25), Guanyuanshu (U.B. 26), Zhibian (U.B. 54), Huantiao (G.B. 30), Yinmen (U.B. 37), Weizhong (U.B. 40), Yanglingquan (G.B. 34), Xuanzhong (G.B. 39), Kunlun (U.B. 60), Zusanli (St. 36), Sanyinjiao (Sp. 6), Ashi points. For every treatment choose 5-7 points of corresponding painful areas of the affected side.

35. Wei Symptom-Complex (Appendix: Polyneuritis)

Wei symptom-complex indicates flaccid paralysis and motor impairment due to weakness, numbness or muscular atrophy of limbs, mostly occurring in lower limbs.

Differentiation

At the early stage of Wei symptom-complex, it is due to

excessive heat of the lung and stomach caused by invasion of exogenous pathogenic heat which exhausts the body fluid of the lung, leading to malnutrition of skin and hair and lacking moisture of tendons and muscles.

It is generally accompanied by fever, cough, irritability, thirst, scanty and yellow urine, diarrhea, red tongue proper with yellow tongue coating, forceful and rapid pulse. The damp-heat type is caused by an accumulation of heat in the spleen and stomach, leading to malnutrition of tendons and muscles and exhaustion of body fluid caused by over-intake of fatty, sweet and spicy food. It can be complicated with soreness and heaviness of limbs, fever with excessive perspiration, stuffy chest; the affected limbs are aversion to heat in turbid urine, yellow and sticky tongue coating, soft and rapid pulse. In the later stages of Wei symptom-complex, when due to deficiency of the liver and kidney without fever, or in case of delayed treatment leading to a chronic condition, the patient might show symptoms like lusterless complexion, soreness and weakness of the lumbar region, dizziness and vertigo, palpitation, spontaneous sweating, red tongue proper with scanty coating, thready and weak pulse. If it is due to weakness of the spleen and stomach, there would be the symptoms of yellowish complexion, shortness of breath, spontaneous sweating, poor appetite, loose stool, atrophy and swelling of affected limbs, pale tongue proper with white coating, soft and retarded pulse.

Treatment

Method: To clarify the heat by selecting the points of the Yangming channels and to remove damp-heat by using the points of the Taiyin channels of hand and foot. Also tonify the bones and tendons by selecting the points of the Shaoyin and Jueyin channels of foot, using the reducing method of acupuncture.

Prescription: Jianyu (L.I. 15), Quchi (L.I. 11), Hegu (L.I. 4), Yangxi (L.I. 5), Biguan (St. 31), Liangqiu (St. 34), Zusanli (St. 36), Jiexi (St. 41).

171

Points added according to symptoms:

Lung-heat: Chize (Lu.5), Feishu (U.B. 13).

Stomach-heat: Neiting (St. 44), Zhongwan (Ren 12).

Damp-heat: Yinlingquan (Sp. 9), Pishu (U.B. 20).

Yin-deficiency of liver and kidney: Ganshu (U.B. 18), Shenshu (U.B. 23), Xuanzhong (G.B. 39), Yanglingquan (G.B. 34).

Fever: Dazhui (Du 14).

Excessive sweating: Taixi (K. 3), Yinxi (H. 6).

Remarks:

1. Wei symptom-complex is commonly seen in multiple neuritis, sequelae of poliomyelitis, acute myelitis, myasthenia gravis, hysterical paralysis and periodic paralysis.

2. Report abstract: The observation has been done on acupuncture treatment of 252 cases of sequelae of poliomyelitis with one-year duration. Among them, 83 cases were cured (34.9 percent); 33 cases (13.1 percent) were approximately cured; 53 cases (21 percent) had remarkable improvement; 46 cases (18.3 percent) improved; 32 cases (12.7 percent), 17 cases had only one or two treatments.

Appendix: Polyneuritis

Polyneuritis is also known as peripheral neuritis which is a kind of sense impairment appearing symmetrically and distally at four extremities accompanied by flaccid palsy, malnutrition and functional disorders. At the early stage it is similar to "Fixed Bi symptom-complex," at the later stage it seems like "Wei symptom-complex."

Differentiation

This disease is mostly due to obstruction of Qi and blood caused by pathogenic damp-heat invading the four extremities; or due to exhaustion of essence and blood caused by indulgence in alcohol, fatty and spicy food leading to malnutrition of tendons and vessels of four limbs or even numbness, pain, muscular atrophy and functional impairment. Overstrain, wading in the water or exposure to cold is the induced factors of this disease. At the beginning there is weakness of limbs developing fully in

172

a few days and accompanied by muscular atrophy, fever, head-ache, stiffness of the neck, paralysis of the four limbs, or hypom-yotonia and paralysis starting from upper or lower extremities spreading symmetrically to other parts of the body. Symptoms of the distal area are sometimes worse than in the proximal area, or vise versa. The paralysis patient has numbness and tingling in the limbs, lasting together with the weakness of limbs, until they turn into sequelae. The disease condition becomes stable after 2-3 weeks, and patients gradually recover after 1-2 months. Some patients have sequelae in different degrees, such as weakness, atrophy, numbness and weakness of muscles, pale tongue proper with scanty coating, thready and weak pulse.

Treatment

Method: To clear up the damp-heat and regulate the circula-tion of Qi and blood with the reducing method of acupuncture at early stage, to reinforce Qi and blood and to relax muscles and tendons with acupuncture and moxibustion at later stage.

Prescription: Jianyu (L.I. 15), Quchi (L.I. 11), Waiguan (S.J. 5), Hegu (L.I. 4), Baxie (Extra), Yangchi (S.J. 4), Yanglao (S.I. 6), Houxi (S.I. 3), Shaohai (H. 3), Huantiao (G.B. 30), Yanglingquan (G.B. 34), Xuanzhong (G.B. 39), Sanyinjiao (Sp. 6), Taibai (Sp. 3), Lougu (Sp. 7), Zusanli (St. 36), Jiexi (St. 41), Bafeng (Extra). For every treatment choose 4-6 points, once every two days.

36. Dysmenorrhea

Dysmenorrhea indicates lower abdominal pain with pain to the low back occurring before, during or after the menses period.

Differentiation

1. Cold-damp stoppage type

Cold pain appears before or during the menses period due to excessive cold drinking, long time sitting or lying on a wet place that injure the lower Jiao and causing pathogenic cold-damp to accumulate in the uterus leading to unsmooth menstrual flow and pain. Pain which can be aggravated by pressure while alle-viated after receiving warmth is accompanied by pain at the back, scanty and dark color menses with clots, thin and white tongue coating, deep and tense pulse.

2. Liver-Qi stagnation type

It is due to liver-Qi stagnation obstructing the blood circulation and blocking the Chong and Ren channels and accumulating in the uterus. The symptoms are: distension and pain of the lower abdomen before or during the menses period (distension is worse than pain), scanty amount with clots, distension and pain in the chest and hypochondriac regions, dark red tongue proper or with stasis spots on the tongue surface, thin and red tongue coating, deep and wiry pulse.

3. Deficiency of kidney and liver

This is due to weak constitution and deficiency of the kidney and liver caused by multiparity and exhaustion of essence and blood. Therefore, during the menstruation, the "sea of blood" becomes empty and fails to nourish the uterus, which causes the pain. It is a dull pain of the lower abdomen during or after menses. The pain is relieved by pressure. Other manifestations are soreness aching of the low back, dizziness, ringing in the ears, pale complexion, lassitude, light color and thin menses, pale tongue proper, deep and thready pulse.

Treatment

1. Cold-damp stoppage type

Method: To warm the coldness and remove dampness, to regulate menses and stop pain by selecting the points of the Ren and Foot-Taiyin channels with acupuncture and moxibustion.

Prescription: Zhongji (Ren 3), Shuidao (St. 28), Diji (Sp. 8).

Points added according to symptoms:

Severe pain: Ciliao (U.B. 32), Guilai (St. 29).

Abdominal pain spreading to the back: Mingmen (Du 4), Shenshu (U.B. 23).

2. Liver-Qi stagnation type

Method: To remove Qi stagnation and regulate Qi circulation and menstruation by selecting the points of the Ren and Jueyin channels with the reducing method of acupuncture.

Prescription: Qihai (Ren 6), Taichong (Liv. 3), Sanyinjiao (Sp. 6).

174

Points added according to the symptoms:
Abdominal distension: Tianshu (St. 25), Qixue (K. 13), Diji
(Sp. 8).
Hypochondriac pain: Yanglingquan (G.B. 34), Guangming
(G.B. 37).
Stuffy chest: Neiguan (P. 6).
3. Deficiency of liver and kidney
Method: To reinforce the liver and kidney and regulate the
functions of the Ren and Chong channels by selecting the points
of the Ren and Foot-Shaoyin channels with the reinforcing
method.
Prescription: Ganshu (U.B. 18), Shenshu (U.B. 23), Guanyuan
(Ren 4), Zusanli (St. 36), Zhaohai (K. 6).
Points added according to the symptoms:
Dizziness and vertigo: Xuanzhong (G.B. 39), Taixi (K. 3).
Abdominal pain: Dahe (K. 12), Qixue (K. 13).
Remarks:
1. Dysmenorrhea which is caused by anteflexion or retroflex-
ion of the uterus, callus (cervical) stenosis, pelvic inflammation, endometriosis, etc., can be treated according to the above-
mentioned differentiation.
2. Emotional stress or physical strain, exposure to cold or
over-intake of cold and raw food should be avoided.
3. A clinical observation of acupuncture treatment for 33
cases of dysmenorrhea: Among them 29 cases had severe pain
and 4 cases had moderate pain. The average disease duration was
longer than 3 years. The points used for observation were: Sanyinjiao (Sp. 6), Zusanli (St. 36), Qihai (Ren 6), Guanyuan (Ren 4),
Zhongji (Ren 3), Qugu (Ren 2), Tianshu (St. 25), Fujie (Sp. 14),
Shenshu (U.B. 23), Ciliao (U.B. 32), Zhongliao (U.B. 33), Hegu (L.I.
4). Among all the points, Sanyinjiao (Sp. 6) together with Guanyuan (Ren 4) or Zhongji (Ren 3) were mostly used in the treatment.
Method: Insert the needle by rotation, retention of needles was
30-60 minutes. Moxibustion was applied for 10-20 minutes after
withdrawal of the needles. The proper time of acupuncture

treatment should be given 1 or 2 days before the menses when the patient had low back pain and lower abdominal pain, once every day or every other day.

Effectiveness: Among all the patients observed, 7 of them were cured, 5 cases had remarkable improvement, 1 case had symptoms relieved. The average time of treatment was 3.9 times. The average application of moxibustion was 2.5 times.

37. Amenorrhea

Amenorrhea indicates the absence of menstrual flow among young women over 18 years old or the absence of menstrual flow continuously for more than three months neglecting the already formed menses cycle. The absence of menses which appears during pregnancy, nursing period, and menopause do not belong to the scope of amenorrhea. It can be classified into Xu and Shi types.

Differentiation

1. Xu type

It is due to emptiness or insufficiency of the "sea of blood" leading to malnutrition of the Chong and Ren channels caused by (1) congenital deficiency of kidney Qi; (2) multiparity consuming essence and blood; (3) improper diet and overstrain injuring the spleen and stomach leading to insufficient formation of blood; (4) severe and chronic disease especially hemorrhagic illness damaging and exhausting Qi and blood. The absence of menses due to complete exhaustion of blood may occur during menopause or after scanty menstruation with delayed cycle. If this is accompanied by dizziness, ringing of the ears, soreness and weakness of the lower back and knees, dry mouth and throat, hotness of palms and soles with irritability, afternoon fever with perspiration, red tongue proper, wiry and thready pulse, these would be the signs of liver and kidney of deficiency. If it is complicated with palpitation, shortness of breath, lassitude, weakness of the extremities, poor appetite, loose stool, pale tongue proper, thready and weak pulse, these are symptoms of spleen and stomach weakness. If it is accompanied by pale and lusterless complexion, dry skin, emaciation, light tongue proper, thready pulse, these are signs of great blood exhaustion.

2. Shi type

This is due to obstruction of the Chong and Ren channels and stoppage of related uterus channels caused by liver-Qi stagnation leading to dysfunction of Qi and blood stasis; or by exogenous pathogenic cold attacking the uterus due to cold drinking or exposure to cold leading to blood stagnation; or by pathogenic phlegm-damp produced by malfunction of transformation and transportation of the spleen obstructing in Chong and Ren channels. If it is manifested by the absence of menses, mental depression, irritability and hot temper, fullness and distension of the chest and hypochondriac regions; lower abdominal pain, dark red or purple tongue proper, or with red spots, deep and wiry pulse, this would indicate Qi stagnation and blood stasis. If the symptoms are cold extremities, cold pain of the lower abdomen with preference for warmth, white tongue coating, deep and slow pulse, this indicates the condition of Qi stagnation and blood stasis. If the symptoms are cold extremities, cold pain of the lower abdomen with preference for warmth, white tongue coating, deep and slow pulse, this is sequel to accumulation of coldness and stagnation of blood. If there are symptoms of fullness and stuffiness of the chest and hypochondriac regions, general fatigue, excessive leukorrhea, fat body-build, sticky tongue coating, slippery pulse, these are caused by accumulation of phlegm-damp.

Treatment

1. Amenorrhea caused by complete exhaustion of blood (Xu type)

Method: To reinforce Qi and nourish blood by selecting the points of the Ren Channel and Back-Shu points of the urinary bladder channel with the reinforcing method of acupuncture and with moxibustion.

Prescription: Ganshu (U.B. 18), Pishu (U.B. 20), Geshu (U.B. 17), Shenshu (U.B. 23), Guanyuan (Ren 4), Zusanli (St. 36),

Sanyinjiao (Sp. 6).

Points added accordingly:

Soreness and pain of the lower back and knee: Mingmen (Du 4), Yaoyan (Extra), Yingu (K. 10).

Afternoon fever and night sweating: Gaohuangshu (U.B. 43), Rangu (K. 2).

Anorexia: Neiguan (P. 6).

2. Amenorrhea caused by blood stagnation (Shi type)

Method: To regulate the Qi function of the liver, build up spleen to dissolve phlegm, warm the channels so as to disperse cold by selecting the points of the Ren channel and Foot-Taiyin channel with the reducing method and with moxibustion.

Prescription: Zhongji (Ren 3), Diji (Sp. 8), Hegu (L.I. 4), Sanyinjiao (Sp. 6), Taichong (Liv. 3), Fenglong (St. 40).

Points added accordingly:

Distension of lower abdomen: Qihai (Ren 6), Siman (K. 14).

Distension and fullness of chest and hypochondriac region: Qimen (Liv. 14), Zhigou (S.J. 6).

Lower abdominal pain: strong moxibustion on Guanyuan (Ren 4), Zhongji (Ren 3).

Excessive leukorrhea: Ciliao (U.B. 32).

Remarks:

1. Amenorrhea which is caused by ovariopathy or endocrine disorders can be treated according to the above-mentioned differentiation.

2. Report of clinical observation of acupuncture treatment for 17 cases of amenorrhea showed the following result: 9 cases were cured, 3 cases had remarkable improvement, 4 cases had a certain degree of improvement, 1 case had no result.

The points used were: Mingmen (Du 4), Shenshu (U.B. 23), Dachangshu (U.B. 25), Changqiang (Du 1), Hegu (L.I. 4), Sanyinjiao (Sp. 6), Diji (Sp. 8), Xuehai (Sp. 10), Siman (K. 14), Dahe (K. 12), Guanyuan (Ren 4), Qugu (Ren 2), Guilai (St. 29), Kunlun (U.B. 60), 4-5 of these points were used for one treatment, once every other day.

3. There are many factors which may cause amenorrhea such as anemia, tuberculosis, nephritis or cardiac diseases. Therefore

necessary examinations should be made before acupuncture treatment in order to find out the clear cause of amenorrhea. Amenorrhea should be also differentiated from early pregnancy.

38. Symptom-Complex Before and After Menopause

It means the symptoms occurring during the cessation of menstruation between the ages of 45 and 50. It is quite often accompanied by physical manifestations, including irregular menstruation, dizziness, palpitation, irritability, perspiration and emotional disturbance. It can be classified into various types according to different causative factors and symptoms.

Differentiation

1. Liver-Yang preponderance type

It is due to kidney-Yin deficiency. Kidney-Yang loses its function of storing essence leading to liver-Yang preponderance. It is manifested by dizziness, vertigo, irritability, exasperation, hot flushes, perspiration, weakness and soreness of the lower back and knees, excessive menstruation, or dribbling of blood, red tongue proper, wiry, thready and rapid pulse.

2. Consumption of heart-blood

This is caused by overstrain of heart that injures and exhausts the heart blood. It has symptoms such as palpitation, anxiety, insomnia, dream-disturbed sleep, hotness of palms and soles, irritability. Or even emotional lability, red tongue proper with scanty coating, thready and rapid pulse.

3. Weakness of spleen and stomach

This is caused by kidney-Yang deficiency. It makes the kidney lose warmth and nourishment from Yin, leading to the weakness of the spleen and stomach. The symptoms are pale and lusterless complexion, general lassitude, poor appetite, abdominal distension, loose stool, swelling of the face and extremities, pale tongue proper and thin coating, deep, thready and forceless pulse.

4. Phlegm accumulation

This is due to dysfunction of transportation and transformation leading to obstruction of phlegm-damp. The symptoms are: fat body-build, stuffy chest with excessive sputum, distension and fullness of the epigastric and abdominal regions, belching, acid regurgitation, nausea and vomiting, poor appetite, swelling, loose stool, sticky tongue coating, and slippery pulse.

Treatment

1. Liver-Yang preponderance

Method: Pacifying liver-Yang and nourish the water in order to compose the wood, puncturing the points of the Foot-Jueyin and Foot-Shaoyin channels with reinforcing and reducing methods accordingly.

Prescription: Taichong (Liv. 3), Taixi (K. 3), Baihui (Du 20), Fengchi (G.B. 20).

Points added according to symptoms:

Irritability: Daling (P. 7).

Hot flushes: Yongquan (K. 1), Zhaohai (K. 6).

Sore-aching of lower back: Shenshu (U.B. 23), Yaoyan (Extra).

2. Deficiency and exhaustion of heart-blood

Method: To reinforce the heart blood and harmonize the heart with the kidney by selecting mainly the Back-Shu points with the reinforcing method of acupuncture or moxibustion.

Prescription: Xinshu (U.B. 15), Pishu (U.B. 20), Shenshu (U.B. 23), Sanyinjiao (Sp. 6).

Points added according to symptoms:

Insomnia: Shenmen (H. 7), Sishencong (Extra).

Palpitation: Tongli (H. 5).

Hotness of palms and soles with irritability: Laogong (P. 8).

Mental disorder: Renzhong (Du 26), Daling (P. 7).

3. Weakness of spleen and stomach

Method: To build up spleen and nourish stomach by puncturing the points of three Yin channels of Foot and Back-Shu points combining with Front-Mu points with reinforcing method and moxibustion.

Prescription: Pishu (U.B. 20), Weishu (U.B. 21), Zhongwan (Ren 12), Zhangmen (Liv. 13), Zusanli (St. 36).

Points added according to the symptoms:

Abdominal distension: Xiawan (Ren 10), Qihai (Ren 6).

Loose stool: Tianshu (St. 25), Yinlingquan (Sp. 9).

Edema: Guanyuan (Ren 4), Shuifen (Ren 9), Zusanli (St. 36).

4. Accumulation of phlegm

Method: To regulate Qi circulation and remove phlegm by puncturing the points of the Ren, Foot-Yangming and Foot-Taiyin channels with the reducing method.

Prescription: Shanzhong (Ren 17), Zhongwan (Ren 12), Qihai (Ren 6), Zhigou (S.J. 6), Fenglong (St. 40), Sanyinjiao (Sp. 6).

Remarks:

1. The above-mentioned methods of treatment are also suitable for climacteric syndrome.

2. the observation of acupuncture treatment for 30 cases of climacteric syndrome:

Main points: Dazhui (Du 14), Guanyuan (Ren 4), Qihai (Ren 6), Zhongwan (Ren 12), Shenshu (U.B. 23), Hegu (L.I. 4), Zusanli (St. 36).

Secondary points: Qugu (Ren 2), Yintang (Extra).

Method of puncturing: Apply the needling according to the order of the above main and secondary points only with the reinforcing method. Retain the needles for 20-30 minutes. Treatment was given every day or every two days.

Effectiveness: 27 cases were cured and 3 cases showed improvement.

39. Uterine Bleeding

Uterine bleeding in Chinese is "Beng Lou," "Beng" indicates abrupt and excessive bleeding of uterus, "Lou" means a dribbling of blood from uterus. Since they can transform into each other during the process of the disease, they are named together as "Beng Lou," translated generally as uterus bleeding. It can be differentiated into Xu and Shi type.

Differentiation

1. Xu type

It is due to Xu (deficiency) of the spleen leading to Qi deficiency and resulting in disorders of the Chong and Ren channels or due to kidney-Yang Xu (deficiency) and kidney-Yin

Xu (deficiency). If excessive bleeding or dribbling of blood is accompanied by pale and lusterless complexion, lassitude, shortness of breath, poor appetite, pale tongue proper with thin and white coating, thready and weak pulse, these are signs of Qi deficiency. If it is Yang deficiency, there would be light red menses, cold pain of the lower abdomen, warmlessness of the four extremities, preference for hotness and fear of cold, loose stool, pale tongue proper with white coating, deep and thready pulse. If it is Yin deficiency, the symptoms would be scanty menses with bright red color, dizziness and ringing in the ears, hotness of palms and soles with irritability, insomnia, night-sweating, weakness and sore-aching of the low back and knees, red tongue proper with scanty coating, thready and rapid pulse.

2. Shi type

If excessive bleeding of the uterus is accompanied by deep red color, foul smell, thickness in quality, thirst with preference for drinking, irritability and hot temper, red tongue proper with yellow coating, slippery and rapid pulse, this indicates heat in blood. If the color of blood is dark red and accompanied by excessive leukorrhea in light yellow or yellow-greenish color with foul smell, pudendal itching and pain, yellow and sticky tongue coating, soft and rapid pulse, this would be the condition which is caused by pathogenic damp-heat. If it is complicated by pain and distension of the chest and hypochondriac regions, irritability and hot temper, tendency of sighing, wiry and rapid pulse, this condition would be due to accumulation of heat. If there are symptoms, such as menses with clots, abdominal pain, pain relieved by discharge of blood clots, dark red tongue proper, deep and rough pulse, these indicate blood stasis.

Treatment

1. Shi type

Method: To disperse heat from the blood for the type of heat in blood; to remove damp-heat for the damp-heat type; to regulate liver-Qi circulation for the Qi-stagnation type; to dislodge the blood stasis and readjust the blood circulation for blood stasis

type, by puncturing the points of the Ren and Foot-Taiyin channels with the reducing method.

Prescription: Qihai (Ren 6), Sanyinjiao (Sp. 6), Yinbai (Sp. 1).
Points added according to different types:

Heat in blood: Xuehai (Sp. 10), Shuiquan (K. 5).

Damp-heat: Zhongji (Ren 3), Yinlingquan (Sp. 9).

Qi stagnation: Taichong (Liv. 3), Zhigou (S.J. 6), Dadun
(Liv. 1).

Blood stasis: Diji (Sp. 8), Qichong (St. 30), Chongmen (Sp. 12).
Points added according to symptoms:

Fever: Dazhui (Du 14), Quchi (L.I. 11).

Irritability: Jianshi (P. 5).

Excessive Leukorrhea: Xialiao (U.B. 34).

Pudendal itching and pain: Ligou (Liv. 5), Xuehai (Sp. 10).

Pain and distension of the chest and hypochondriac regions:
Shanzhong (Ren 17), Qimen (Liv. 14), Yanglingquan (G.B. 34).

Abdominal pain unable to stand pressure: Hegu (L.I. 4),
Zhongji (Ren 3), Siman (K. 14).

2. Xu type

Method: To reinforce Qi of the middle Jiao for Qi Xu (deficiency); to warm and tonify the Yang for Yang Xu (deficiency);
to strengthen the kidney-Yin for Yin Xu (deficiency), by puncturing the points of the Ren, Foot-Taiyin and Foot-Shaoyin channels with the reinforcing method. Moxibustion is advisable.

Prescription: Guanyuan (Ren 4), Sanyinjiao (Sp. 6), Shenshu
(U.B. 23), Jiaoxin (K. 8).

Points added according to different types:

Qi Deficiency: Qihai (Ren 6), Pishu (U.B. 20), Gaohuangshu
(U.B. 43), Zusanli (St. 36).

Yang Xu (deficiency): Qihai (Ren 6), Mingmen (Du 4), Fuliu
(K. 7).

Yin Xu: Rangu (K. 2), Yingu (K. 10).

Points added according to symptoms:

Loose stool: Tianshu (St. 25).

Insomnia: Shenmen (H. 7).

Night sweating: Yinxi (H. 6).

Weakness and soreness of the lower back and knees: Yaoyan

Remarks:

Functional uterine bleeding or uterine bleeding caused by some other factors can also be treated according to the above method.

40. Excessive Leukorrhea

Under normal conditions, there is a small amount of white discharge in the vagina to moisten and protest the vaginal surface. Excessive leukorrhea means there is more vaginal discharge than normal. This symptom may be a physiological change or a pathological change. The excessive leukorrhea due to physiological change is seen during adolescence, pregnancy and the premenstrual period and is manifested by white and thin discharge without offensive smell. The excessive leukorrhea due to pathological change is common with the inflammation of the genital organs, weak body constitution or excessive sexual irritation. Those factors which can increase the local congestion of the genital organs may induce excessive discharge of the vagina.

Traditional Chinese medicine holds that excessive leukorrhea is the manifestation of excessive pathogenic dampness pouring downward. It can be classified into the cold damp and heat damp types. Heat damp type is characterized by yellow color, thick and sticky with the offensive smell of leukorrhea accompanied by hot temper, anxiety, and yellow-sticky tongue coating. The cold damp type has the feature of white discharge, thin and clear leukorrhea, and pale tongue proper with white coating. Both types are complicated by soreness and aching of the lower back.

Treatment

Main points: Daimai (G.B. 26), Qihai (Ren 6), Qugu (Ren 2), Sanyinjiao (Sp. 6).

Combined points: Guanyuan (Ren 4), Zusanli (St. 36).

Method: First puncture Daimai (G.B. 26), Qugu (Ren 2) and Sanyinjiao (Sp. 6). If it is the heat damp type, Xingjian (Liv. 2) and Yinlingquan (Sp. 9) can be added. While Guanyuan (Ren 4) and Zusanli (St. 36) can be added together with moxibustion for the cold damp type.

41. Hysteria

Hysteria is characteristic by hyperactivity of some parts of the nervous system. It is similar to "Zangzao" in traditional Chinese medicine. It is commonly seen among young women with acute onset and clear psychological factors. The clinical manifestations are changeable and complicated, such as convulsive hysteria; hysteric paralysis mostly affecting limbs; spasms and contractions; loss of sensations, loss of voice, blindness, deafness, insanity, emotional lability, talking nonsense, trance, etc. Clinical examination shows no organic pathological changes.

Treatment

Main Points: Renzhong (Du 26), Yongquan (K. 1), Neiguan (P. 6), Shenmen (H. 7), Zhongchong (P. 9).

Method: Puncture one or two of the above points with swift insertion and withdrawal of needles and give a strong stimulation for patients with schizophrenia. The following points can be supplemented:

Paralysis: Quchi (L.I. 11), Huantiao (G.B. 30), Yanglingquan (G.B. 34).

Spasms and convulsion similar to the seizure of epilepsy: Houxi (S.I. 3), Hegu (L.I. 4), Taichong (Liv. 3), Yanglingquan (G.B. 34).

Aphasia: Tongli (H. 5), Yamen (Du 15), Lianquan (Ren 23). Deafness: Tinghui (G.B. 2), Yifeng (S.J. 17), Hand-Zhongzhu (S.J. 3).

Blindness: Jingming (U.B. 1).

Hiccough: Zhongwan (Ren 12), Zusanli (St. 36).

Globus hystericus: Tiantu (Ren 22).

Trismus: Hegu (L.I. 4), Jiache (St. 6).

Typical case 1: Female, 25 years of age.

"She suddenly exhibited mental disorder on New Year's Eve of 1959, talking nonsense and confusion to the people about her. Soon afterwards she was sent to the hospital where acupuncture treatment was given on Zhongchong (P. 9) with strong stimulation and swift insertion and withdrawal of the needle. The patient became clear minded as usual, and left with a less weakness of the body."

Case 2: Female, 24 years of age.

"She had sudden syncope after receiving news of the death of her mother. She went into convulsion for 2 hours, then cried, laughed, shouted, refused to eat food and had a sleepless night. She was unable to cooperate with the doctor who examined her in the clinic. Examination only showed corneal congestion; there were no other abnormalities. She was diagnosed as 'hysteric twilight state.' At 8 o'clock of the same night when she was hospitalized, she was given an intramuscular injection of 0.1 g. luminal sodium, falling asleep afterwards. She started to have trouble again at 11 o'clock. Acupuncture treatment was given on Renzhong (Du 26), Hegu (L.I. 4) and Yongquan (K. 1) with strong stimulation. The patient was cured after one treatment, and discharged from the hospital on the 5th day."

42. Urticaria

Urticaria, also known as "wind wheals," is a kind of allergic skin disease. The attack appears to be connected with physical, chemical or biological factors to which the patient is hypersensitive. An abrupt onset has itching wheals of various sizes or with pimples rising one after another in white or light red color, red skin around the rashes, causing terrible itching. The attack may pass off in a few minutes or a few hours, or may last for several days. The eruption continues to come out in excessive patches.

Treatment

Main points: Quchi (L.I. 11), Xuehai (Sp. 10), Zusanli (St. 36), Weizhong (U.B. 40).

Combined points: Sanyinjiao (Sp. 6), Geshu (U.B. 17), Zhongwan (Ren 12), Neiguan (P. 6).

Method: Puncture first on Quchi (L.I. 11), Xuehai (Sp. 10) and Zusanli (St. 36) during the attack of urticaria. It is accompanied by stomachache or irritability. Neiguan (P. 6) and Zhongwan (Ren 12) can be used. If it is bright red in color, Geshu (U.B. 17) should be added, or venous pricking on Quchi (L.I. 11) with a three-edged needle. Zusanli (St. 36) has a particularly good effect on urticaria caused by food allergens.

43. Alopecia

Alopecia areata is also known as "devil shaving head" in Chinese. The etiology is not clear. Usually it is caused by great mental stress, or great anxiety, or sudden nervous shock. Clinically the hair falls off in patches or complete balding, or even the loss of body hair like eyebrows, beard, arm pit and pubic hair in severe cases. Traditional Chinese medicine holds that this is due to Yin deficiency of the liver and kidney leading to malnutrition of the hair.

Treatment

Use plum-blossom needle to tap slightly the affected area and making it become congested, red and bleeding for 5-10 minutes. after tapping with plum-blossom acupuncture, rub the skin of balding area with raw and fresh ginger.

Typical case: Female, 40 years of age.

"She came to the hospital in July 1985 because of hair loss in patches. She complained that she had the same condition two years ago, and was cured by plum-blossom acupuncture. Recently, she began to have alopecia areata resulting in shiny, smooth bald areas. The sizes of the bald areas varied from 0.5 to 2 cm. in diameter. She was treated again with plum-blossom needle once every two days. After three weeks' treatment, there was new hair coming out from the bald areas."

Appendix

Fourteen Channels and Their Acupuncture Points

I. The Lung Channel of Hand-Taiyin

Zhongfu (Lu. 1)

Yunmen (Lu. 2)

Tianfu (Lu. 3)

Xiabai (Lu. 4)

Chize (Lu. 5)

Kongzui (Lu. 6)

Lieque (Lu. 7)

Jingqu (Lu. 8)

Taiyuan (Lu. 9)

Yuji (Lu. 10)

Shaoshang (Lu. 11)

II. The Large Intestine Channel of Hand-Yangming

Shangyang (L.I. 1)

Erjian (L.I. 2)

Sanjian (L.I. 3)

Hegu (L.I. 4)

Yangxi (L.I. 5)

Pianli (L.I. 6)

Wenliu (L.I. 7)

Xialian (L.I. 8)

Shanglian (L.I. 9)

Shousanli (L.I. 10)

Quchi (L.I. 11)

Zhouliao (L.I. 12)

Hand-Wuli (L.I. 13)

Binao (L.I. 14)

Jianyu (L.I. 15)

Jugu (L.I. 16)

Tianding (L.I. 17)

Neck-Futu (L.I. 18)

Nose-Heliao (L.I. 19)

Yingxiang (L.I. 20)

III. The Stomach Channel of Foot-Yangming

Chengqi (St. 1)

Sibai (St. 2)

Nose-Juliao (St. 3)

Dicang (St. 4)

Daying (St. 5)

Jiache (St. 6)

Xiaguan (St. 7)

Touwei (St. 8)

Renying (St. 9)

Shuitu (St. 10)

Qishe (St. 11)

Quepen (St. 12)

Qihu (St. 13)

Kufang (St. 14)

Wuyi (St. 15)

Yingchuang (St. 16)

Ruzhong (St. 17)
Rugen (St. 18)
Burong (St. 19)
Chengman (St. 20)
Liangmen (St. 21)
Guanmen (St. 22)
Taiyi (St. 23)
Huaroumen (St. 24)
Tianshu (St. 25)
Wailing (St. 26)
Daju (St. 27)
Shuidao (St. 28)
Guilai (St. 29)
Qichong (St. 30)
Biguan (St. 31)

Femur-Futu (St. 32)
Yinshi (St. 33)
Liangqiu (St. 34)
Dubi (St. 35)
Zusanli (St. 36)
Shangjuxu (St. 37)
Tiaokou (St. 38)
Xiajuxu (St. 39)
Fenglong (St. 40)
Jiexi (St. 41)
Chongyang (St. 42)
Xiangu (St. 43)
Neiting (St. 44)
Lidui (St. 45)

IV. The Spleen Channel of Foot-Taiyin

Yinbai (Sp. 1)
Dadu (Sp. 2)
Taibai (Sp. 3)
Gongsun (Sp. 4)
Shangqiu (Sp. 5)
Sanyinjiao (Sp. 6)
Lougu (Sp. 7)
Diji (Sp. 8)
Yinlingquan (Sp. 9)
Xuehai (Sp. 10)
Jimen (Sp. 11)

Chongmen (Sp. 12)
Fushe (Sp. 13)
Fujie (Sp. 14)
Daheng (Sp. 15)
Fuai (Sp. 16)
Shidou (Sp. 17)
Tianxi (Sp. 18)
Xiongxiang (Sp. 19)
Zhourong (Sp. 20)
Dabao (Sp. 21)

V. The Heart Channel of Hand-Shaoyin

Jiquan (H. 1)
Qingling (H. 2)
Shaohai (H. 3)
Lingdao (H. 4)
Tongli (H. 5)

Yinxi (H. 6)
Shenmen (H. 7)
Shaofu (H. 8)
Shaochong (H. 9)

VI. The Small Intestine Channel of Hand-Taiyang

Shaoze (S.I. 1)
Qiangu (S.I. 2)
Houxi (S.I. 3)
Hand-Wangu (S.I. 4)
Yanggu (S.I. 5)
Yanglao (S.I. 6)
Zhizheng (S.I. 7)
Xiaohai (S.I. 8)
Jianzhen (S.I. 9)
Naoshu (S.I. 10)

Tianzong (S.I. 11)
Bingfeng (S.I. 12)
Quyuan (S.I. 13)
Jianwaishu (S.I. 14)
Jianzhongshu (S.I. 15)
Tianchuang (S.I. 16)
Tianrong (S.I. 17)
Quanliao (S.I. 18)
Tinggong (S.I. 19)

VII. The Urinary Bladder Channel of Foot-Taiyang

Jingming (U.B. 1)
Zanzhu (U.B. 2)
Meichong (U.B. 3)
Quchai (U.B. 4)
Wuchu (U.B. 5)
Chengguang (U.B. 6)
Tongtian (U.B. 7)
Luoque (U.B. 8)
Yuzhen (U.B. 9)
Tianzhu (U.B. 10)
Dashu (U.B. 11)
Fengmen (U.B. 12)
Feishu (U.B. 13)
Jueyinshu (U.B. 14)
Xinshu (U.B. 15)
Dushu (U.B. 16)
Geshu (U.B. 17)
Ganshu (U.B. 18)
Danshu (U.B. 19)
Pishu (U.B. 20)

Weishu (U.B. 21)
Sanjiaoshu (U.B. 22)
Shenshu (U.B. 23)
Qihaishu (U.B. 24)
Dachangshu (U.B. 25)
Guanyuanshu (U.B. 26)
Xiaochangshu (U.B. 27)
Pangguangshu (U.B. 28)
Zhonglushu (U.B. 29)
Baihuanshu (U.B. 30)
Shangliao (U.B. 31)
Ciliao (U.B. 32)
Zhongliao (U.B. 33)
Xialiao (U.B. 34)
Huiyang (U.B. 35)
Chengfu (U.B. 36)
Yinmen (U.B. 37)
Fuxi (U.B. 38)
Weiyang (U.B. 39)
Weizhong (U.B. 40)

Fufen (U.B. 41)
Pohu (U.B. 42)
Gaohuangshu (U.B. 43)
Shentang (U.B. 44)
Yixi (U.B. 45)
Geguan (U.B. 46)
Hunmen (U.B. 47)
Yanggang (U.B. 48)
Yishe (U.B. 49)
Weicang (U.B. 50)
Huangmen (U.B. 51)
Zhishi (U.B. 52)
Baohuang (U.B. 53)
Zhibian (U.B. 54)

Heyang (U.B. 55)
Chengjin (U.B. 56)
Chengshan (U.B. 57)
Feiyang (U.B. 58)
Fuyang (U.B. 59)
Kunlun (U.B. 60)
Pushen (U.B. 61)
Shenmai (U.B. 62)
Jinmen (U.B. 63)
Jinggu (U.B. 64)
Shugu (U.B. 65)
Foot-Tonggu (U.B. 66)
Zhiyin (U.B. 67)

VIII. The Kidney Channel of Foot Shaoyin

Yongquan (K. 1)
Rangu (K. 2)
Taixi (K. 3)
Dazhong (K. 4)
Shuiquan (K. 5)
Zhaohai (K. 6)
Fuliu (K. 7)
Jiaoxin (K. 8)
Zhubin (K. 9)
Yingu (K. 10)
Henggu (K. 11)
Dahe (K. 12)
Qixue (K. 13)
Siman (K. 14)

Abdomen-Zhongzhu (K. 15)
Huangshu (K. 16)
Shangqu (K. 17)
Shiguan (K. 18)
Yindu (K. 19)
Abdomen-Tonggu (K. 20)
Youmen (K. 21)
Bulang (K. 22)
Shenfeng (K. 23)
Lingxu (K. 24)
Shencang (K. 25)
Yuzhong (K. 26)
Shufu (K. 27)

IX. The Pericardium Channel of Hand-Jueyin

Tianchi (P. 1)
Tianquan (P. 2)

Quze (P. 3)
Ximen (P. 4)

Jianshi (P. 5)
Neiguan (P. 6)
Daling (P. 7)

Laogong (P. 8)
Zhongchong (P. 9)

X. The Sanjiao Channel of Hand-Shaoyang

Guanchong (S.J. 1)
Yemen (S.J. 2)
Hand-Zhongzhu (S.J. 3)
Yangchi (S.J. 4)
Waiguan (S.J. 5)
Zhigou (S.J. 6)
Huizong (S.J. 7)
Sanyangluo (S.J. 8)
Sidu (S.J. 9)
Tianjing (S.J. 10)
Qinglengyuan (S.J. 11)
Xiaoluo (S.J. 12)

Naohui (S.J. 13)
Jianliao (S.J. 14)
Tianliao (S.J. 15)
Tianyou (S.J. 16)
Yifeng (S.J. 17)
Qimai (S.J. 18)
Luxi (S.J. 19)
Jiaosun (S.J. 20)
Ermen (S.J. 21)
Ear-Heliao (S.J. 22)
Sizhukong (S.J. 23)

XI. The Gall Bladder Channel of Foot-Shaoyang

Tongziliao (G.B. 1)
Tinghui (G.B. 2)
Shangguan (G.B. 3)
Hanyan (G.B. 4)
Xuanlu (G.B. 5)
Xuanli (G.B. 6)
Qubin (G.B. 7)
Shuaigu (G.B. 8)
Tianchong (G.B. 9)
Fubai (G.B. 10)
Head-Qiaoyin (G.B. 11)
Head-Wangu (G.B. 12)
Benshen (G.B. 13)
Yangbai (G.B. 14)
Head-Linqi (G.B. 15)

Muchuang (G.B. 16)
Zhengying (G.B. 17)
Chengling (G.B. 18)
Naokong (G.B. 19)
Fengchi (G.B. 20)
Jianjing (G.B. 21)
Yuanye (G.B. 22)
Zhejin (G.B. 23)
Riyue (G.B. 24)
Jingmen (G.B. 25)
Daimai (G.B. 26)
Wushu (G.B. 27)
Weidao (G.B. 28)
Femur-Juliao (G.B. 29)
Huantiao (G.B. 30)

Fengshi (G.B. 31)

Femur-Zhongdu (G.B. 32)

Xiyangguan (G.B. 33)

Yanglingquan (G.B. 34)

Yangjiao (G.B. 35)

Waiqiu (G.B. 36)

Guangming (G.B. 37)

Yangfu (G.B. 38)

Xuanzhong (G.B. 39)

Qiuxu (G.B. 40)

Foot-Linqi (G.B. 41)

Diwuhui (G.B. 42)

Xiaxi (G.B. 43)

Foot-Qiaoyin (G.B. 44)

XII. The Liver Channel of Foot-Jueyin

Dadun (Liv. 1)

Xingjian (Liv. 2)

Taichong (Liv. 3)

Zhongfeng (Liv. 4)

Ligou (Liv. 5)

Foot-Zhongdu (Liv. 6)

Xiguan (Liv. 7)

Ququan (Liv. 8)

Yingbao (Liv. 9)

Femur-Wuli (Liv. 10)

Yinlian (Liv. 11)

Jimai (Liv. 12)

Zhangmen (Liv. 13)

Qimen (Liv. 14)

XIII. The Ren Channel

Huiyin (Ren 1)

Qugu (Ren 2)

Zhongji (Ren 3)

Guanyuan (Ren 4)

Shimen (Ren 5)

Qihai (Ren 6)

Abdomen-Yinjiao (Ren 7)

Shenque (Ren 8)

Shuifen (Ren 9)

Xiawan (Ren 10)

Jianli (Ren 11)

Zhongwan (Ren 12)

Shangwan (Ren 13)

Juque (Ren 14)

Jiuwei (Ren 15)

Zhongting (Ren 16)

Shanzhong (Ren 17)

Yutang (Ren 18)

Chest-Zigong (Ren 19)

Huagai (Ren 20)

Xuanji (Ren 21)

Tiantu (Ren 22)

Lianquan (Ren 23)

Chengjiang (Ren 24)

XIV. The Du Channel

Changqiang (Du 1)

Yaoshu (Du 2)

Yaoyangguan (Du 3)
Mingmen (Du 4)
Xuanshu (Du 5)
Jizhong (Du 6)
Zhongshu (Du 7)
Jinsuo (Du 8)
Zhiyang (Du 9)
Lingtai (Du 10)
Shendao (Du 11)
Shenzhu (Du 12)
Taodao (Du 13)
Dazhui (Du 14)
Yamen (Du 15)

Fengfu (Du 16)
Naohu (Du 17)
Qiangjian (Du 18)
Houding (Du 19)
Baihui (Du 20)
Qianding (Du 21)
Xinhui (Du 22)
Shangxing (Du 23)
Shenting (Du 24)
Suliao (Du 25)
Renzong (Du 26)
Duiduan (Du 27)
Mouth-Yinjiao (Du 28)

A Glossary of the Acupuncture Points

Abdomen-Tonggu (腹通谷 K. 20)

Abdomen-Yinjiao (阴交 Ren 7)

Abdomen-Zhongzhu (中注 K. 15)

Baihuanshu (白环俞 U.B. 30)

Baihui (百会 Du 20)

Baohuang (胞肓 U.B. 53)

Benshen (本神 G.B. 13)

Biguan (髀关 St. 31)

Binao (臂臑 L.I. 14)

Bingfeng (秉风 S.I. 12)

Bulang (步廊 K. 22)

Burong (不容 St. 19)

Changqiang (长强 Du 1)

Chengfu (承扶 U.B. 36)

Chengguang (承光 U.B. 6)

Chengjiang (承浆 Ren 24)

Chengjin (承筋 U.B. 56)

Chengling (承灵 G.B. 18)

Chengman (承满 St. 20)

Chengqi (承泣 St. 1)

Chengshan (承山 U.B. 57)

Chest-Zigong (紫宫 Ren 19)

Chize (尺泽 Lu. 5)

Chongmen (冲门 Sp. 12)

Chongyang (冲阳 St. 42)

Ciliao (次髎 U.B. 32)

Dabao (大包 Sp. 21)

Dachangshu (大肠俞 U.B. 25)

Dadu (大都 Sp. 2)

Dadun (大敦 Liv. 1)

Dahe (大赫 K. 12)

Daheng (大横 Sp. 15)

Daimai (带脉 G.B. 26)

Daju (大巨 St. 27)

Daling (大陵 P. 7)

Danshu (胆俞 U.B. 19)

Dazhu (大杼 U.B. 11)

Daying (大迎 St. 5)

Dazhong (大钟 K. 4)

Dazhui (大椎 Du 14)

Dicang (地仓 St. 4)

Diji (地机 Sp. 8)

Diwuhui (地五会 G.B. 42)

Dubi (犊鼻 St. 35)

Duiduan (兑端 Du 27)

Dushu (督俞 U.B. 16)

Ear-Heliao (和髎 S.J. 22)

Erjian (二间 L.I. 2)

Ermen (耳门 S.J. 21)

Feishu (肺俞 U.B. 13)

Feiyang (飞扬 U.B. 58)

Femur-Futu (伏兔 St. 32)

Femur-Juliao (居髎 G.B. 29)

Femur-Wuli (足五里 Liv. 10)

Femur-Zhongdu (中渎 G.B. 32)

Fengchi (风池 G.B. 20)

Fengfu (风府 Du 16)

Fenglong (丰隆 St. 40)

Fengmen (风门 U.B. 12)

Fengshi (风市 G.B. 31)

Foot-Linqi (足临泣 G.B. 41)

Foot-Qiaoyin (足窍阴 G.B. 44)

Foot-Tonggu (足通谷 U.B. 66)

Foot-Zhongdu (中都 Liv. 6)

Fuai (腹哀 Sp. 16)

Fubai (浮白 G.B. 10)

Fufen (附分 U.B. 41)

Fujie (腹结 Sp. 14)

Fuliu (复溜 K. 7)

Fushe (府舍 Sp. 13)

Fuxi (浮郄 U.B. 38)

Fuyang (跗阳 U.B. 59)

Ganshu (肝俞 U.B. 18)

Gaohuangshu (膏肓俞 U.B. 43)

Geguan (膈关 U.B. 46)

Geshu (膈俞 U.B. 17)

Gongsun (公孙 Sp. 4)

Guanchong (关冲 S.J. 1)

Guangming (光明 G.B. 37)

Guanmen (关门 St. 22)

Guanyuan (关元 Ren 4)

Guanyuanshu (关元俞 U.B. 26)

Guilai (归来 St. 29)

Hand-Wangu (腕骨 S.I. 4)

Hand-Wuli (手五里 L.I. 13)

Hand-Zhongzhu (中渚 S.J. 3)

Hanyan (颔厌 G.B. 4)

Head-Linqi (头临泣 G.B. 15)

Head-Qiaoyin (头窍阴 G.B. 11)

Head-Wangu (完骨 G.B. 12)

Hegu (合谷 L.I. 4)

Henggu (横骨 K. 11)

Heyang (合阳 U.B. 55)

Houding (后顶 Du 19)

Houxi (后溪 S.I. 3)

Huagai (华盖 Ren 20)

Huangmen (肓门 U.B. 51)

Huangshu (肓俞 K. 16)

Huantiao (环跳 G.B. 30)

Huaroumen (滑肉门 St. 24)

Huiyang (会阳 U.B. 35)

Huiyin (会阴 Ren 1)

Huizong (会宗 S.J. 7)

Hunmen (魂门 U.B. 47)

Jiache (颊车 St. 6)

Jianjing (肩井 G.B. 21)

Jianli (建里 Ren 11)

Jianliao (肩髎 S.J. 14)

Jianshi (间使 P. 5)

Jianwaishu (肩外俞 S.I. 14)

Jianyu (肩髃 L.I. 15)

Jianzhen (肩贞 S.I. 9)

Jianzhongshu (肩中俞 S.I. 15)

Jiaosun (角孙 S.J. 20)

Jiaoxin (交信 K. 8)

Jiexi (解溪 St. 41)

Jimai (急脉 Liv. 12)

Jimen (箕门 Sp. 11)

Jinggu (京骨 U.B. 64)

Jingmen (京门 G.B. 25)

Jingming (睛明 U.B. 1)

Jingqu (经渠 Lu. 8)

Jinmen (金门 U.B. 63)

Jinsuo (筋缩 Du 8)

Jiquan (极泉 H. 1)

Jiuwei (鸠尾 Ren 15)

Jizhong (脊中 Du 6)

Jueyinshu (厥阴俞 U.B. 14)

Jugu (巨骨 L.I. 16)

Juque (巨阙 Ren 14)

Kongzui (孔最 Lu. 6)

Kufang (库房 St. 14)

Kunlun (昆仑 U.B. 60)

Laogong (劳宫 P. 8)

Liangmen (梁门 St. 21)

Liangqiu (梁丘 St. 34)

Lianquan (廉泉 Ren 23)

Lidui (厉兑 St. 45)

Lieque (列缺 Lu. 7)

Ligou (蠡沟 Liv. 5)

Lingdao (灵道 H. 4)

Lingtai (灵台 Du 10)

Lingxu (灵墟 K. 24)

Lougu (漏谷 Sp. 7)

Luoque (络却 U.B. 8)

Luxi (颅息 S.J. 19)

Meichong (眉冲 U.B. 3)

Mingmen (命门 Du 4)

Mouth-Yinjiao (龈交 Du 28)

Muchuang (目窗 G.B. 16)

Naohu (脑户 Du 17)

Naohui (臑会 S.J. 13)

Naokong (脑空 G.B. 19)

Naoshu (臑俞 S.I. 10)

Neck-Futu (扶突 L.I. 18)

Neiguan (内关 P. 6)

Neiting (内庭 St. 44)

Nose-Heliao (禾髎 L.I. 19)

Nose-Juliao (巨髎 St. 3)

Pangguangshu (膀胱俞 U.B. 28)

Pianli (偏历 L.I. 6)

Pishu (脾俞 U.B. 20)

Pohu (魄户 U.B. 42)

Pushen (仆参 U.B. 61)

Qianding (前顶 Du 21)

Qiangjian (强间 Du 18)

Qiangu (前谷 S.I. 2)

Qichong (气冲 St. 30)

Qihai (气海 Ren 6)

Qihaishu (气海俞 U.B. 24)

Qihu (气户 St. 13)

Qimai (瘛脉 S.J. 18)

Qimen (期门 Liv. 14)

Qinglengyuan (清冷渊 S.J. 11)

Qingling (青灵 H. 2)

Qishe (气舍 St. 11)

Qiuxu (丘墟 G.B. 40)

Qixue (气穴 K. 13)

Quanliao (颧髎 S.I. 18)

Qubin (曲鬓 G.B. 7)

Quchai (曲差 U.B. 4)

Quchi (曲池 L.I. 11)

Quepen (缺盆 St. 12)

Qugu (曲骨 Ren 2)

Ququan (曲泉 Liv. 8)

Quyuan (曲垣 S.I. 13)

Quze (曲泽 P. 3)

Rangu (然谷 K. 2)

Renying (人迎 St. 9)

Renzong (人中 Du 26)

Riyue (日月 G.B. 24)

Rugen (乳根 St. 18)

Ruzhong (乳中 St. 17)

Sanjian (三间 L.I. 3)

Sanjiaoshu (三焦俞 U.B. 22)

Sanyangluo (三阳络 S.J. 8)

Sanyinjiao (三阴交 Sp. 6)

Shangguan (上关 G.B. 3)

Shangjuxu (上巨虚 St. 37)

Shanglian (上廉 L.I. 9)

Shangliao (上髎 U.B. 31)

Shangqiu (商丘 Sp. 5)

Shangqu (商曲 K. 17)

Shangwan (上脘 Ren 13)

Shangxing (上星 Du 23)

Shangyang (商阳 L.I. 1)

Shanzhong (膻中 Ren 17)

Shaochong (少冲 H. 9)

Shaofu (少府 H. 8)

Shaohai (少海 H. 3)

Shaoshang (少商 Lu. 11)

Shaoze (少泽 S.I. 1)

Shencang (神藏 K. 25)

Shendao (神道 Du 11)

Shenfeng (神封 K. 23)

Shenmai (申脉 U.B. 62)

Shenmen (神门 H. 7)

Shenque (神阙 Ren 8)

Shenshu (肾俞 U.B. 23)

Shentang (神堂 U.B. 44)

Shenting (神庭 Du 24)

Shenzhu (身柱 Du 12)

Shidou (食窦 Sp. 17)

Shiguan (石关 K. 18)

Shimen (石门 Ren 5)

Shousanli (手三里 L.I. 10)

Shuaigu (率谷 G.B. 8)

Shufu (俞府 K. 27)

Shugu (束骨 U.B. 65)

Shuidao (水道 St. 28)

Shuifen (水分 Ren 9)

Shuiquan (水泉 K. 5)

Shuitu (水突 St. 10)

Sibai (四白 St. 2)

Sidu (四渎 S.J. 9)

Siman (四满 K. 14)

Sizhukong (丝竹空 S.J. 23)

Suliao (素髎 Du 25)

Taibai (太白 Sp. 3)

Taichong (太冲 Liv. 3)

Taixi (太溪 K. 3)

Taiyi (太乙 St. 23)

Taiyuan (太渊 Lu. 9)

Taodao (陶道 Du 13)

Tianchi (天池 P. 1)

Tianchong (天冲 G.B. 9)

Tianchuang (天窗 S.I. 16)

Tianding (天鼎 L.I. 17)

Tianfu (天府 Lu. 3)

Tianjing (天井 S.J. 10)

Tianliao (天髎 S.J. 15)

Tianquan (天泉 P. 2)

Tianrong (天容 S.I. 17)

Tianshu (天枢 St. 25)

Tiantu (天突 Ren 22)

Tianxi (天溪 Sp. 18)

Tianyou (天牖 S.J. 16)

Tianzhu (天柱 U.B. 10)

Tianzong (天宗 S.I. 11)

Tiaokou (条口 St. 38)

Tinggong (听宫 S.I. 19)

Tinghui (听会 G.B. 2)

Tongli (通里 H. 5)

Tongtian (通天 U.B. 7)

Tongziliao (瞳子髎 G.B. 1)
Touwei (头维 St. 8)
Waiguan (外关 S.J. 5)
Wailing (外陵 St. 26)
Waiqiu (外丘 G.B. 36)
Weicang (胃仓 U.B. 50)
Weidao (维道 G.B. 28)
Weishu (胃俞 U.B. 21)
Weiyang (委阳 U.B. 39)
Weizhong (委中 U.B. 40)
Wenliu (温溜 L.I. 7)
Wuchu (五处 U.B. 5)
Wushu (五枢 G.B. 27)
Wuyi (屋翳 St. 15)
Xiabai (侠白 Lu. 4)
Xiaguan (下关 St. 7)
Xiajuxu (下巨虚 St. 39)
Xialian (下廉 L.I. 8)
Xialiao (下髎 U.B. 34)
Xiangu (陷谷 St. 43)
Xiaochangshu (小肠俞 U.B. 27)
Xiaohai (小海 S.I. 8)
Xiaoluo (消泺 S.J. 12)
Xiawan (下脘 Ren 10)
Xiaxi (侠溪 G.B. 43)
Xiguan (膝关 Liv. 7)
Ximen (郄门 P. 4)
Xingjian (行间 Liv. 2)
Xinhui (囟会 Du 22)
Xinshu (心俞 U.B. 15)
Xiongxiang (胸乡 Sp. 19)
Xiyangguan (膝阳关 G.B. 33)
Xuanji (璇玑 Ren 21)
Xuanli (悬厘 G.B. 6)

Xuanlu (悬颅 G.B. 5)
Xuanshu (悬枢 Du 5)
Xuanzhong (悬钟 G.B. 39)
Xuehai (血海 Sp. 10)
Yamen (哑门 Du 15)
Yangbai (阳白 G.B. 14)
Yangchi (阳池 S.J. 4)
Yangfu (阳辅 G.B. 38)
Yanggang (阳纲 U.B. 48)
Yanggu (阳谷 S.I. 5)
Yangjiao (阳交 G.B. 35)
Yanglao (养老 S.I. 6)
Yanglingquan (阳陵泉 G.B. 34)
Yangxi (阳溪 L.I. 5)
Yaoshu (腰俞 Du 2)
Yaoyangguan (腰阳关 Du 3)
Yemen (液门 S.J. 2)
Yifeng (翳风 S.J. 17)
Yinbai (隐白 Sp. 1)
Yinbao (阴包 Liv. 9)
Yindu (阴都 K. 19)
Yingchuang (膺窗 St. 16)
Yingu (阴谷 K. 10)
Yingxiang (迎香 L.I. 20)
Yinlian (阴廉 Liv. 11)
Yinlingquan (阴陵泉 Sp. 9)
Yinmen (殷门 U.B. 37)
Yinshi (阴市 St. 33)
Yinxi (阴郄 H. 6)
Yishe (意舍 U.B. 49)
Yixi (譩譆 U.B. 45)
Yongquan (涌泉 K. 1)
Youmen (幽门 K. 21)
Yuanye (渊腋 G.B. 22)

Yuji (鱼际 Lu. 10)

Yunmen (云门 Lu. 2)

Yutang (玉堂 Ren 18)

Yuzhong (彧中 K. 26)

Yuzhen (玉枕 U.B. 9)

Zanzhu (攒竹 U.B. 2)

Zhangmen (章门 Liv. 13)

Zhaohai (照海 K. 6)

Zhejin (辄筋 G.B. 23)

Zhengying (正营 G.B. 17)

Zhibian (秩边 U.B. 54)

Zhigou (支沟 S.J. 6)

Zhishi (志室 U.B. 52)

Zhiyang (至阳 Du 9)

Zhiyin (至阴 U.B. 67)

Zhizheng (支正 S.I. 7)

Zhongchong (中冲 P. 9)

Zhongfeng (中封 Liv. 4)

Zhongfu (中府 Lu. 1)

Zhongji (中极 Ren 3)

Zhongliao (中髎 U.B. 33)

Zhonglüshu (中膂俞 U.B. 29)

Zhongshu (中枢 Du 7)

Zhongting (中庭 Ren 16)

Zhongwan (中脘 Ren 12)

Zhouliao (肘髎 L.I. 12)

Zhourong (周荣 Sp. 20)

Zhubin (筑宾 K. 9)

Zusanli (足三里 St. 36)

图书在版编目（CIP）数据

实用针灸：英文/耿俊英、苏志红著．

－北京：新世界出版社,1998.7 重印

ISBN 7 – 80005 – 115 – 3

I.实··· II.①耿···②苏 III.针灸疗法－英文 IV.R245

实用针灸

编　　著：耿俊英　苏志红

责任编辑：张民捷

出　　版：新世界出版社

社　　址：北京百万庄路 24 号

邮政编码：100037

电　　话：0086 – 10 – 68326645（出版发行部）

传　　真：0086 – 10 – 68326679

经　　销：新华书店

印　　刷：北京大学印刷厂

开　　本：787 × 1092 毫米 1/16 开本

印　　张：13

版　　次：1991 年（英文）第 1 版　　1998 年北京第 3 次印刷

书　　号：ISBN 7 – 80005 – 115 – 3/R · 040

定　　价：30 元